The ABCs of
International Finance

The ABCs of
International Finance

Understanding the Trade and Debt Crisis

John Charles Pool
Charles Pool & Associates

Steve Stamos
Bucknell University

Lexington Books
D.C. Heath and Company/Lexington, Massachusetts/Toronto

Library of Congress Cataloging-in-Publication Data

Pool, John Charles.
    The ABCs of international finance.

    Bibliography: p.
    Includes index.
        1. International finance. 2. Balance of payments. 3. Debts, External—Developing
countries. 4. International economic relations. I. Stamos, Steve, 1947-   . II. Title.
HG3851.P66   1987   332′.042   86-45933
ISBN 0-669-15605-1 (alk. paper)
ISBN 0-669-14601-3 (pbk. : alk. paper)

Published simultaneously in Canada
Printed in the United States of America
Casebound International Standard Book Number: 0-669-15605-1
Paperbound International Standard Book Number: 0-669-14601-3
Library of Congress Catalog Card Number: 86-45933

The paper used in this publication meets the minimum requirements of American National
Standard for Information Sciences—Permanence of Paper for Printed Library Materials,
ANSI Z39.48-1984. ∞™

87 88 89 90 8 7 6 5 4 3 2 1

Contents

Tables

Figures

Preface

This is a time when interest in business and economics seems to be growing at an increasing rate. Economics classes are oversubscribed. Everyone, it seems, wants to learn how to make money.

It is also a time of general optimism in the business world. By the fall of 1986 the United States had entered its fifth year of sustained growth. The stock market is booming; inflation seems under control; interest rates are low; and unemployment—while still high by historical standards—seems to have stabilized. There is a sense of calmness and optimism in the air.

Yet it is an uneasy calm. We find students and businesspeople perplexed by news of record high trade deficits and the concomitant loss of the U.S. industrial sector to foreign competition; by the news that the United States has now become a debtor nation; and by the very real possibility that Third World underdeveloped countries will be unable to pay their debts. *Default* has become a household word.

The economics textbooks don't have an explanation for all this. There is, in our view, a void in the literature on international economics that can be used in the classroom. We hope to fill that void by providing an up-to-date analysis of the international financial sector in a historical context—the twentieth century—and by using basic microeconomic principles and relevant examples to develop the essential concepts and principles of international trade and finance. We have emphasized the following major policy issues:

1. The fluctuation of the U.S. dollar from the mid-1970s to the late 1980s.

2. The impact and consequences of the OPEC oil embargo in 1973–74, the doubling of oil prices in 1979, the oil glut and softening of oil prices in 1981–85, and the collapse of oil prices in 1986.

3. The origins and emergence of the Third World debt crisis, Mexico's near default in 1982, the role of the International Monetary Fund, stabilization policies, and the consequences of development.

4. The changing composition of U.S. trade, the direction of U.S. trade, U.S. trade deficits, the overall U.S. balance of payments, and U.S. competitiveness. Case studies include the steel, automobile, and agriculture sectors.

We believe that this book is suitable for students in a variety of courses. While international economics is the most obvious, we also envision its use in intermediate macro theory, economic development, and even introductory economics courses. The book is written in simple, nontechnical language, but it neither trivializes the international sector, as introductory textbooks usually do, nor does it mathematize the subject, which is the approach of most advanced texts. Therefore, the book is appropriate for students at many levels. We hope it helps them understand how, in the real world of the 1980s, there is no such thing as a national economy any more—virtually everything depends on the smooth functioning of the international economy.

Acknowledgments

Like all books, this one is a result of many people's efforts. Our ideas and perspectives have been influenced by more people than could reasonably be listed here, but among them are: Jorge Castenada, John C. Chitwood, Norris Clement, James Crotty, Ross M. LaRoe, John Hodges, Harry Magdoff, Robert Rafferty, Tom Riddell, and Frank E. Wagner.

We also gratefully acknowledge the efforts of Alice Van Buskirk and Linda Vollmer, who "processed" the words through many drafts with patience and persistence far beyond what could have been expected. Also, many thanks to Martha Thorp, who provided very important editorial input.

And, of course, we appreciate our families, Betty, Mike, and Laura Linda; Lucy, Barry, and Lisanna, who understand.

The ABCs of
International Finance

1
Introduction

One of the most complicated areas in all of economics is international trade theory and its facilitating mechanism, international finance. Trade is easier to conceptualize: we make things and trade them to other countries, other countries do the same, and everybody gains. But the manner in which this process is financed is something few people understand, and even most of them can't (or won't) explain it.

Until recently, most businesspeople felt they could afford to ignore the intricacies of international finance—it was something best handled by the Swiss bankers, the gnomes of Zurich. But as the world has become increasingly internationalized and interdependent, no one nowadays can escape the vicissitudes of international finance. We're all in this together.

Consider the following:

By August 1986, the unemployment rate in the United States was 6.8 percent; but, in Aliquippa, Pennsylvania, just north of Pittsburgh, over 13 percent were unemployed. The economic recovery that spread across the nation between 1983 and 1986 missed Aliquippa completely. Its steel plant, which had employed over 12,000 workers several years previously, employed only 800 in 1986. What happened in Aliquippa happened throughout Pennsylvania. In 1976, there were over 200,000 jobs in the steel and primary metals industry in the state, but by 1986, less than 100,000 remained.

To protect himself against a sharply devalued currency, Venezuelan businessman Jose-Manuel Sanchez sold 20 million bolivars worth of stock in Venezuelan companies and with the proceeds bought $1 million worth of certificates of deposit from Chemical Bank in New York, depositing the rest in a West German bank.

In 1981, petroleum was selling for $32.50 a barrel. U.S. oil fields were crowded with geologists and drilling rigs. But by August 1986, petroleum prices had collapsed to $12.50 a barrel and the oil fields had become symbols of debt, bankruptcy, and unemployment. Texas alone faced a $3.2 billion state budget deficit and an unemployment rate of almost 12 percent.

In 1986 a USX steel worker on strike complained that after accepting a $3 per hour reduction in wages and benefits two years previously, the company was now demanding another cut of $5.50 per hour in wages and benefits. Without this concession from the union workers, the company claimed, it could not compete against foreign steel producers and would be forced to shut down.

A formerly unemployed machinist from Chicopee, Massachusetts, is now working in a new high tech industry located off Route 128 outside Boston. While he is delighted to be working, he made $4.85 an hour in 1986 in his new job, compared to $9.75 an hour in his former job. To make ends meet, his wife is working at a fast-food restaurant for $3.35 an hour.

Just off of Interstate 90 in the middle of Minnesota, in a small breakfast diner, a poster tacked to the wall above the cash register reads, "FUTURE FARMERS OF AMERICA: WHO NEEDS THEM?"

An Iowa farmer who has just lost his farm wearily contemplates the irony of his misfortune: his overproduction of corn contributed to declining grain prices and eventually the foreclosure of his farm. As he reads the evening newspaper, he sees that so much grain was produced over the past year that there is no place to store it. On another page is a story about famine and starvation in East Africa, and below that story he reads that the president has offered to sell wheat to the Soviet Union at a 30 percent discount. Even at that price, the Russians aren't buying. They can get it cheaper elsewhere. Unable to comprehend the interdependence of these seemingly unrelated stories, he reflects on his new job in a service station—owned by his wife's brother.

Mexican peasant Maria Nunez, a mother of eleven children, discovered one morning that tortillas, the main staple of her family's diet, had doubled in price during the past six months. She was informed that the government had further reduced its food subsidy. The reduction had something to do with deficits, debt, and a loan from the International Monetary Fund in Washington, D.C.—which is a long way from her small farm in Santa Cruz just outside of Guadalajara.

In Rochester, New York, a Kodak production line worker with twenty-two years of seniority is laid off. Competition from the Japanese, he is told, is the reason. What, he wonders, as he drives his Toyota to the unemployment office, has become of the American dream?

The reason international finance is affecting our lives in such a dramatic way is that through an unusual set of circumstances, the U.S. banking system—the strongest in the world—has become extremely vulnerable to disaster, if not to a total collapse.

Ironically, this all came about because of the strength of the U.S. economy after World War II and the subsequent adoption of the U.S. dollar as the world's key currency. Since then, the dollar has replaced gold as the medium of exchange for international transactions and has become the reserve currency for most nations. Therefore, anything that threatens the health of the U.S. dollar also threatens the health, if not the very existence, of world trade and, as such, everyone's well-being.

The seeds of the present crisis were sown when the Organization of Petroleum Producing Countries (OPEC) was able to establish a near monopoly of the world's oil supply and increased oil prices by 1,700 percent over the 1971–73 period. Industrialized countries dependent on petroleum had no option but to pay the price, leading to one of the largest transfers of wealth in history. Oil continued to flow to the West and several hundred billion dollars (nicknamed *petrodollars*) flowed back to the Middle East in payment for it. The OPEC countries, in turn, were not able to absorb such a large infusion of funds without risking runaway inflation, so they simply deposited the money in the safest logical place: the banks of the industrialized world.

Now the banks had an unusual but not unattractive problem—what to do with these unexpected new deposits. Banks survive and prosper by loaning out deposits at a rate higher than they pay for them. Given the recession of the mid-1970s (caused in part by the oil price shock), the only seemingly qualified borrowers were the countries of the Third World, which were in need of capital.

Therefore, on the now dubious, but then seemingly logical assumption that governments don't go bankrupt and, consequently, are good credit risks, billions of dollars were transferred to the Third World. By 1986, this debt amounted to nearly one trillion dollars. These loans seemed to make sense in the beginning because almost everyone believed that transferring capital to where it was needed was simply good economics. It seemed so logical that even the International Monetary Fund made considerable efforts to facilitate the process. A new phrase even entered our vocabulary to describe it: *petrodollar recycling*.

But such an assumption is valid only if the borrowing countries are able to invest the funds in economic activities that produce a rate of return higher than the rate of interest on the loans. Unfortunately, this didn't happen.

Private banks, in their somewhat unaccustomed new role as international development bankers, didn't have the resources, the know-how, or the authority to monitor how their loans were used. As a result, much of the money simply disappeared, was transferred into personal accounts (often right back at the banks from where the money came), or was invested in ill-conceived pork barrel development projects.

By the late 1970s, the debtor countries began to realize that their export capacity was not sufficient to continue meeting their debt obligations (which were compounding at an increasing rate). Refinancing became commonplace.

Then, in August 1982, the Mexican government announced that it could no longer service its debt. For all practical purposes, Mexico was bankrupt. This sent a shock through the international financial system, especially since Mexico was a major oil producer and was, therefore, assumed to be one of the most creditworthy of the debtor nations. In a near panic atmosphere, the banking authorities quickly arranged a temporary bailout, rescheduling the Mexican debt. The crisis was averted, at least temporarily.

Since then, the general situation has become even more precarious: Argentina, Brazil, and most of the debtor countries have been forced to reschedule their mounting debts. The banks have had little option but to accommodate them and, thus, reluctantly pour good money after bad. To make matters worse, by 1985, the ten major U.S. banks were exposed to the Third World debtor countries by more than 200 percent of their net worth making a default by *even one* of the major debtor countries enough to almost certainly trigger a banking panic, a run on the banks, and a potential collapse of the U.S. banking system.

In 1986, the breakup of OPEC, the accompanying declining oil prices, and an unexpected dramatic fall of interest rates seemed at first to signal the end of the crisis. Most of the debtor countries are also oil importers so it appeared that they would be able to more easily service their debts. Lower interest rates also relieved some pressure as the debts were rescheduled at lower rates. Some of the debtor countries, notably Argentina and Brazil, saw their position improve somewhat.

However, some of the oil-exporting debtor countries, especially Mexico and Nigeria, now find themselves in a nearly impossible dilemma. Mexico, the more serious case, receives 70 percent of its export earnings from oil. Mexico owes about $100 billion, $25 billion of that directly to U.S. private banks. Without oil revenues (as we shall show), there is no way Mexico can continue to service its debt over the long run. Therefore, while lower oil prices would in general appear to be good news for everyone, they may well push Mexico into bankruptcy. This alone could be enough to precipitate a crisis in the U.S. banking system.

Understanding this ironic turn of events requires an understanding of the role of the dollar in international finance, the theoretical subtleties and the realities of international trade, and the mechanics of international lending. These issues are the subject of this book. After they have been examined in some detail, we then take up the question of why previous policy prescriptions have failed and we suggest some possible solutions to this increasingly pressing problem.

Chapter 2 takes up the question of international trade and demonstrates how and why everyone gains from specializing and trading. However, trade is directly related to the method of financing it. Because of the general acceptability of the U.S. dollar, the United States has for many years been able to run huge balance of trade deficits, buying much more from abroad than it is selling. In 1985, the U.S. trade deficit amounted to more than $150 billion; this is historically unprecedented.

Unfortunately, the U.S. economy is also beset with problems from other directions: *stagflation* (inflation coupled with stagnating growth in production), strong competition from foreign manufacturers, and the banking system's vulnerability to Third World nations' debt. Chapter 3 looks at these woes using the ailing steel and farm industries as examples. It then assesses the Carter and Reagan administrations' efforts to get the economy moving again despite stagflation and trade deficits.

Any time any country has a trade deficit, financial transactions must take place to balance and accommodate the difference; otherwise, such a deficit couldn't occur. In order to understand why this is such an important aspect of the present situation, one must realize that there is an important difference between the theory of exchange rate adjustments that are supposed to prevent such imbalances and the reality of the present world economic situation in which no such adjustment has occurred. Therefore, in chapter 3, we examine the various systems of exchange rate determination and how—theoretically—they are supposed to function.

A key point here is that in recognition of the fact that the huge U.S. trade deficits can't continue forever without creating an even more serious crisis, the major Free World industrialized nations (the Group of Five—United States, France, Japan, Great Britain, and West Germany) have recently abandoned the free-flexible exchange rate system (which had been in place since 1973) in favor of a coordinated market intervention to control the value of the dollar in relation to other currencies, notably the Japanese yen.

As was planned, this intervention has caused the dollar to fall somewhat and has stimulated U.S. exports. But this in turn has merely worsened the problem and contributed to the fragility of the system. The weaker dollar has reduced incentives for foreign investors to invest in the U.S. Their investment was the factor that brought equilibrium to the trade imbalance; it was a major source of financing of the U.S. federal deficit as well.

In chapter 4, we examine and explain the all-important role of the U.S. dollar in the international financial system. If the dollar were not the world's key reserve currency (being used for more than 50 percent of all international transactions), the debt crisis, which is really a dollar crisis, wouldn't have such serious implications for the U.S. economy. A country that allows its currency to be used as a key currency has many privileges, but in broader terms, it also has responsibilities. The collapse of the dollar, like the meltdown of a nuclear power plant, would lead to fallout all over the world and everyone would feel its effects. We shall eventually argue that the United States, which has recently become a debtor nation itself, has a responsibility to see that this doesn't happen.

In chapter 5 we then take up the question of the debt explosion in the U.S. economy and the accompanying demise of the U.S. industrial sector. Over the past two decades, the U.S. economy has been plagued by record federal deficits which have resulted in an internal debt of over $2 trillion, an amount equal to the U.S. Gross National Product.

Moreover, as the rest of the world has become more industrialized, efficient, and competitive the U.S. has lost its once predominant position in the international economy. The U.S. trade deficit has been running at all-time record highs, causing the country—once the world's largest creditor—to become a debtor nation internationally. The consequences of this turn of events are incalculable.

Therefore, we examine this situation is some detail. Then we put it into the context of the most serious problem of all: the vulnerability of the U.S. banking system to the internal and external debt build-up. We then examine the potential consequences of a collapse of the international financial system which would most certainly follow a collapse of the U.S. economy.

Chapter 6 then focuses on the rise of the Eurodollar within the European nations, the petrodollar within the oil-rich Arab world, and one serious net result of all this flux: the Third World debt crisis. The presumed purpose of international lending is to transfer capital from the wealthy industrialized nations to developing Third World nations which have little capital. However, what is occurring now is just the opposite: a net transfer of funds *from* the Third World *to* the industrialized world. This process cannot continue forever without serious economic and political repercussions. The situation is further explained in chapter 7.

In chapter 7, we take up the case of Mexico. In our view, the Mexican economy is on the verge of collapse and there is nothing in present policy that will reverse this increasingly likely possibility. The economic and political pressures on the Mexican government to declare itself in default are growing. If that happens, the Western world could be facing a financial crisis of unprecedented proportions. Therefore, we examine the precarious Mexican situation in some detail.

Then, in chapter 8, we examine the more general debt crisis in a policy context. It is not just the Third World that is in a state of debt crisis; it is the entire world. This is because the United States itself is facing a debt crisis of unprecedented proportions.

The U.S. national debt has more than doubled in the 1980s. Business and personal debt now amount to more than $4 *trillion*. Total debt in the U.S. economy is more than $6 trillion. In 1985, the U.S. became a debtor nation internationally for the first time since 1914. This means that the United States now owes more to foreign interests than it is owed by them. This external debt—estimated to amount to more than $1 trillion by 1990—will soon become a serious drain on U.S. internal resources.

So, we shall argue, there is a triple debt crisis looming over the international financial system. The staggering Third World debt, coupled with rapidly growing U.S. internal debt *and* U.S. external debt, has precipitated a fragile situation which is not sustainable over the long run.

Economists have described and explained the problem. But solving it will take some enlightened politicians. At this juncture none appear on the horizon.

2
The Role of International Trade

International trade has a long and illustrious history. As far back as classical antiquity, nations have traded. There are several reasons for trade. One is, of course, that everyone gains or at least perceives that they gain from the process. Otherwise, it wouldn't happen. Perhaps a more important reason is that all nations are interdependent. No nation can be self-sufficient—independent from international trade—without great sacrifices.

The United States, for example, is one of the more self-sufficient countries in the world, yet it depends on imports for the large majority of its bauxite, diamonds, tin, coffee, nickel, manganese, rubber, tungsten, bananas, gold, platinum, and chromium. The latter two are crucial in the production of jet engines and many other industrial processes, but they are nonexistent in the United States and come almost exclusively from South Africa.

So every nation needs imports, some albeit more than others. It follows then that if a nation needs imports, it also needs exports because there is no other way to pay for imports. All nations, therefore, need imports *and* exports. In other words, they need international trade. The gains from international trade are the same as the gains from any other kind of trade. When people specialize, productivity is increased. And when they trade, their incomes are higher as is overall consumption.

In one sense, international trade is very simple: each nation specializes in whatever it can produce the most efficiently and trades the resulting product to someone else for whatever it does best. Given that the distribution of skills and national resources is not the same throughout the world, everyone gains from the process. But in another sense, the process is quite complicated. That's because everyone's self-interest is involved.

Chances are you don't make your own shoes or clothing. Instead, you specialize in doing whatever you can do best and you sell your services (your labor) or your product in the marketplace. So either directly or indirectly, you trade with others and both you and they are presumably better off for it. Almost no one—neither nation nor individual—is self-sufficient, and no nation these days tries to get along without international trade. You can understand this better if you try to build an automobile in your garage or grow some bananas in your garden.

This process of specializing and trading was first elaborated in detail by Adam Smith in 1776 in the classic book popularly known as *The Wealth of Nations* (but, in fact, entitled *An Inquiry into the Nature and Causes of the Wealth of Nations*). Smith's work still provides the theoretical foundation and rationale for free-market capitalism.

In some 1,200 pages, Smith elaborated the fact that people gain by pursuing their own self-interest. A private vice—selfishness—becomes a public virtue when people selfishly specialize in doing whatever they can do best, "truck" the result off somewhere and "barter" it (exchange it for something else). The theory of capitalism says that free competition between buyers and sellers assures that the whole process works out to everyone's best interest, and that competition and trade are normal and important parts of the capitalist system.

What is often overlooked is that Smith wrote *The Wealth of Nations* not only as an explanation of how capitalism works but also as a diatribe against the mercantilist trading policies of the eighteenth century nation-states. The mercantilists felt that the primary objective of trading internationally was to export as much as possible and accumulate gold in return. This, they thought, was the "nature and cause" of the wealth of nations.

Not so, said Smith. Nations, as well as individuals, gain from specializing and trading. But Smith's ideal trade wasn't goods for gold, but goods for goods. This set the stage for a controversy which has persisted for more than 200 years now. If Smith was right, as most economists nowadays believe he was, then there is no place in a rational world for protectionist, self-interested measures to restrict trade through artificial barriers such as tariffs and import quotas. As figure 2–1 shows, in 1985, total world exports reached an astounding volume of $1.78 *trillion*, so clearly international trade is no small issue.

Three Theories of International Trade

Various theories explain how international trade does—or should—function. The theories of *absolute advantage* and *comparative advantage* are not controversial. *Protectionism*, however, is hotly debated, for it affects special interest groups much differently than it affects the general public.

The Theory of Absolute Advantage

Refined by Smith's follower, David Ricardo, and dressed up in modern terminology—the ABC s version—the theory of absolute advantage goes like this.

With rare exceptions, almost any nation can produce any two given products. Steel *and* wheat, bananas *and* refrigerators, and guns *and* butter are but a

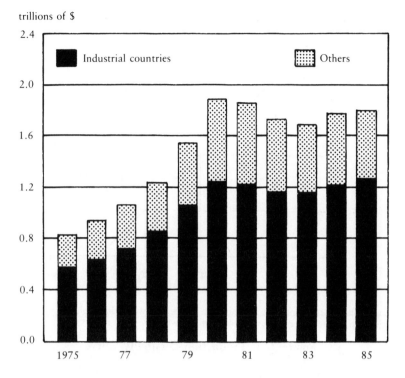

trillions of $

Source: International Monetary Fund.

Figure 2–1. Trends in World Trade, 1975–85

few of the more obvious examples. The same nation can also choose to produce steel *or* wheat, bananas *or* refrigerators, or guns *or* butter. The problem comes in deciding on what combination to produce, since the possibilities are infinite. Figure 2–2 depicts the various combinations possible in producing two goods in one country *without* international trade.

Obviously, if you are efficient at producing steel and need wheat (as, for example, West Germany, Japan, and South Korea do), then you should produce steel and trade it to someone (for example, the United States, Canada, or Argentina, who are efficient at producing wheat). Or if (like Central America) you are efficient at producing bananas, but need refrigerators, then you'll certainly want to leave the production of refrigerators to someone else (such as the United States, which is good at it) and put your efforts into bananas. These are examples of what is called *absolute advantage*. In such a case, everyone gains from specializing and trading internationally.

You can see absolute advantage demonstrated in figure 2–3, which is derived from the data in table 2–1. Using some simplifying assumptions (such as the

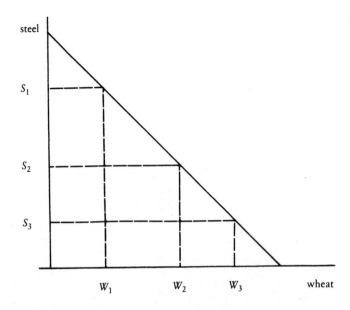

Figure shows various possible combinations of steel and wheat that could be produced, given limited resources and technological know-how.

Figure 2–2. Production Possibility Curve

fact that all present U.S. copper miners would have to become wheat farmers for this to work), we can easily see that the United States has a clear absolute advantage over Chile in wheat production. If all U.S. resources went into wheat production, then it could produce 12 units of wheat, whereas Chile could only produce 3 units. On the other hand, Chile, with its abundant resources, could produce 12 units of copper. But even if it gave up completely on copper and put all of its efforts into producing wheat, it could only produce 3 units of wheat.

Now, since both countries need wheat *and* copper, if no trade exists and each is going it alone, they would have to divide their efforts between the two, let's say, for simplicity, into a 50–50 split. Under those conditions, the United States would be producing 6 units of wheat and 1.5 units of copper. Chile would produce the opposite: 1.5 units of wheat and 6 units of copper. Between the two 7.5 units of wheat and 7.5 units of copper would be produced.

It's obvious by now that each country can gain a lot by specializing in what it does best and trading to the other. If the United States puts all of its effort into wheat production, it can produce 12 units, while if Chile produces only copper, it can produce 12 units. Then they do a bit of trading. The *total* production of wheat and copper is now 12 + 12, or 24 units, whereas without

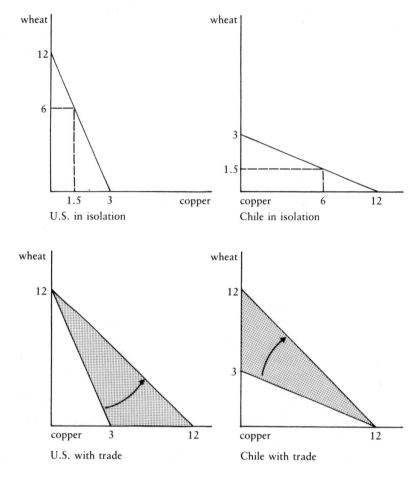

Figure 2–3. Gains from Trade with Absolute Advantage

trade, it was only 7.5 + 7.5, or 15 units. So clearly it would seem that everyone is better off when the two countries specialize and trade.

The point of all this is that countries can gain from specializing and trading. Productivity is increased, incomes are higher because more is sold, costs are lower, and consumption is higher. Everybody gains from international trade when absolute advantages exist, or at least that would certainly seem to be the case.

The Theory of Comparative Advantage

But there's more. What if the United States is more efficient at producing *both* wheat *and* copper? Is there then any reason why the United States should trade

Table 2–1
Production Possibilities for the United States and Chile with and without Trade

Without trade:

	Wheat	*or*	Copper
United States	12		3
Chile	3		12

In isolation trying to produce both:

	Wheat	*and*	Copper
United States	6.0		1.5
Chile	1.5		6.0
Total production	7.5		7.5

Total possible production with trade:

	Wheat	*and*	Copper
United States	12		0
Chile	0		12
Total production	12		12

with Chile? Common sense would tell us there's not. But, as David Ricardo demonstrated in the early 1800s, both countries can still gain from trade so long as even just a comparative advantage exists. To see why, take a look at figure 2–4. Then read on.

Let's think for example about trade between the United States and Argentina. Both are good at producing beef and wheat, yet the two countries still trade beef and wheat, even though the United States is more efficient at producing both. Why? Because with specialization, there are still advantages in trading; otherwise, trade obviously wouldn't occur.

In figure 2–4 we see that the United States can produce 12 units of beef *or* 3 units of wheat. Argentina, however, can produce 2 units of beef or 1 unit of wheat. So if the United States specializes in beef and sells it to Argentina and Argentina specializes in wheat and sells some to the United States, both countries still gain. (This can get complicated. Mostly it's a question of cost ratios. The relative prices are different in the two countries. In the United States, beef and wheat trade at a 4:1 ratio, while in Argentina the beef-wheat cost ratio is 2:1, so—compared to wheat—beef is more expensive in the United States than in Argentina. Therefore, trade still makes sense. By trading, Argentina gets a unit of beef at the U.S. cost of 1/4 unit of wheat, whereas, by producing it at home, it would have cost 1/2 unit of wheat. And the United States gets each unit of wheat at a cost of 1/2 unit of beef whereas producing it at home costs 4 units of beef. This is an oversimplified example, but the principle still holds: both countries gain from trading—in theory.)

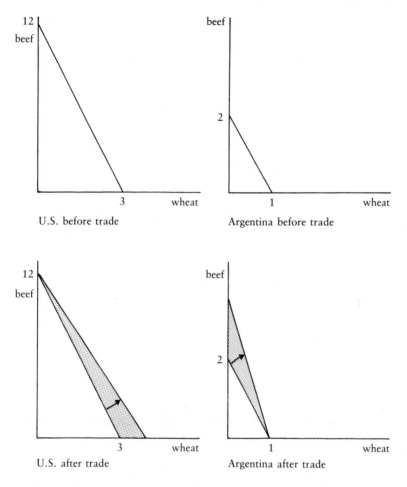

Figure 2–4. Gains from Trade with Comparative Advantage

So economists of almost all pedigrees and all but the most myopic politicians seem to agree that international trade is beneficial to everyone. But it's not that simple. What complicates the issue is the apparently obvious fact that for a system of trading goods internationally to work, there has to be at least some semblance of balance between what is traded (between what is imported and what is exported). Otherwise, someone gets more of the gains than is fair and someone else loses more than is fair.

Again, the analogy of individuals trading in the market is relevant. The idea of trading is to come out ahead. The winners in the exchange process are those who are good "horse traders" or good bargainers. Everyone tries to buy cheap and sell dear. If you win at this game, you can become wealthy;

if you lose, you'll be poor, the point being that there are always winners and losers.

Now, if we extend this logic to the international arena, a similar process occurs. Everyone wants to be a winner, which in this case means every country wants to export more than it imports. In one sense, this is a curious kind of logic because by exporting more than it is importing, a country is sending more of its goods out of the country than it is getting back, which seems a very strange way to improve the general welfare. This is, in fact, why Adam Smith railed against the mercantilists: all you accumulate when you have an export surplus is gold or, more likely, another's currency which is, in the final analysis, just paper.

But what's at issue here is jobs. These days, some 15 percent of the U.S. economy is involved in and dependent on the international sector—exports and imports. For most other regions, especially Japan and Western Europe, that figure is much higher. For example, more than 50 percent of the Japanese economy depends on exports.

So since every country wants to provide more jobs for its people, everyone tries to increase their exports as much as possible, while at the same time limiting imports, which of course costs jobs. The problem, however, is that since one country's exports are another's imports, it is clearly *not possible for everyone* to have an export surplus but, nonetheless, everyone tries. This is why international trade is often called a "beggar-thy-neighbor" game whose object is to make yourself better off at your neighbor's expense.

The Theory of Protectionism

One result of this goal is called "export fetish protectionism." It seems logical enough that if your objective is to maximize exports and minimize imports, then one simple way to do it is to put a tax on imports (a *tariff*) or to limit by law the quantity of imports (a *quota*). Tariffs and quotas have the effect of increasing prices in the domestic industries by protecting them from foreign competition. This *protectionism*, of course, saves jobs at home. However, it also raises a host of problems and is one of the most controversial issues in economics, as we shall see.

The theory of tariffs is fairly simple. Many economists agree that tariffs don't make economic sense (except in the case of a developing country trying to protect an *infant industry*—a new industry still struggling to establish itself). The reason is demonstrated in figure 2–5, which you should look at before you read on. At the top, a standard supply and demand graph shows the conditions that would prevail if a country were in isolation and not trading a product (say, steel) internationally. The price would be P_1 and the quantity sold Q_1.

Now, if the country entered world trade, it would be facing a horizontal (perfectly *elastic*) demand curve, which means it could sell or buy all it wanted at the world price P_2. Note, however, who gains and who loses.

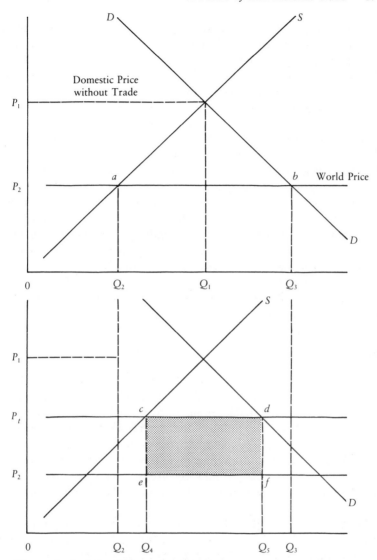

Figure 2–5. The Effect of a Tariff on a Domestic Economy

Consumers gain since they now can buy steel products at the new lower world price P_2. Also, since the law of demand tells us that consumers will buy more at a lower price, we know they probably will; they'll now buy quantity Q_3 at the lower price P_2.

Obviously, in this scenario, domestic producers lose. They were producing and selling quantity Q_1 at price P_1, but now it will only be profitable for them to produce up to quantity Q_2 (the point where the supply line intersects the world price line). The additional supply of steel (Q_2 to Q_3) will be imported, the net result being that a lot of jobs in the domestic steel industry will be lost to foreign competition.

So now protectionism enters the picture. The steel industry lobby puts pressure on Congress to place a tariff on steel imports. The effects of this tariff are demonstrated in the lower graph in figure 2–5.

The tariff raises the domestic price of steel from P_2 to P_t. *Consumers lose because they (or we) have to pay a higher price and will accordingly buy less (as shown by the area from Q_5 to Q_3).* Producers, on the other hand, gain. At the higher price P_t, they will find it profitable to produce up to quantity Q_4, for a gain shown on the graph between Q_2 and Q_4. The rectangle *cdef* represents the tariff, the tax collected by the government on steel imports.

So the net effect of the protectionist tariff is to increase domestic production, to increase steel producer's profits, and to increase employment in the domestic steel industry. The government also gains tax revenues. The losers, of course, are consumers who are subsidizing the steel industry by paying higher prices and obtaining less steel. To put it another way, the effect of a tariff is to redistribute income from consumers in general to the steel producers and their employees and, to a lesser extent, to the government.

Problems of Trade and Tariff Theory

As we have seen, the theory of international trade seems logical enough. Certainly it is attractive and convincing. Tariffs, quotas, and protectionist measures provide a way to correct imbalances and distortions. But, as is often the case in economics, there is one minor problem: they don't work. International trade does, of course, take place, but the theory doesn't explain what actually happens.

The theory of comparative advantage, as we have seen, says that if each nation puts its best foot forward and specializes in what it can do best, everyone will produce and consume more when they trade and everyone will have higher incomes as a result.

The example David Ricardo used when he first proposed this idea was the relationship between Great Britain and Portugal: Britain produced wool, Portugal produced wine, and they traded. Both, according to Ricardo, should gain. However, as one writer has pointed out, that didn't quite happen.

> Britain and Portugal began their partnership in 1373, when they formed an alliance against Castile, the Spanish empire. In 1580, Castile expanded into Portugal. Sixty years later, Britain began to offer Portugal military support against Spain in exchange for a series of economic concessions. A critical concession was made in the Treaty of Methuen, signed in 1703.
>
> According to this treaty, the Portuguese agreed to impose no tariffs on wool cloth and other woolen goods from Britain on the condition that the British lower their duties on wine imported from Portugal to two-thirds of those

currently imposed on imported French wine. Since the British had already lowered the duties on Portuguese wine in 1690, they clearly stood to gain more from the treaty than the Portuguese.

The impact of the Treaty of Methuen on the Portuguese economy was tremendous. British wool exports to Portugal jumped by 120 percent between 1700 and 1710. During the same period, the Portuguese sold 40 percent more wine to the British and wine production expanded fivefold. But the group of small-time Portuguese artisans who made woolen products could hardly compete with the cheap imports of British wool, and were eventually forced to abandon their enterprise.

By the 1850s, Portuguese economic growth had stagnated, and Portugal had become economically dependent on Britain. While the development of the textile industry had laid the foundation for the British Empire, specialization in wine had succeeded in transforming Portugal into what looked like a small South American republic that just happened to be attached to Europe.[1]

Most economics textbooks explain the theory of comparative advantage by using the now fabled example of secretaries and lawyers.[2] Imagine that lawyers can type faster than their secretaries, yet they do the legal work and leave the typing to the secretaries. Why? Because lawyers have a comparative advantage. They can earn more doing the legal work, so (theoretically) between the lawyers and secretaries, their total product is greater, as is their income, than it would be if the lawyers spent less time on legal work and more time typing.

But, of course, it is the lawyers' income that is higher, not the secretaries'. The arrangement is clearly to the lawyers' advantage. However, if the secretaries learned a new skill—such as legal work—they would increase their comparative advantage, their income.

So when we compare two countries trading under conditions of comparative advantage, a similar process usually (but not always) occurs. Most of the time, smaller and/or underdeveloped countries have one or two comparative advantages: abundant, cheap labor or abundant, cheap raw materials (for example, tin in Bolivia, copper in Chile, and oil in Mexico).

If it is the abundant labor that is being traded, then specializing in labor-intensive products (those requiring more labor than capital to produce) merely ensures that labor will remain cheap and incomes low. If incomes rise, the rationale for trade is gone since costs of producing the good will have to rise as well.

The case of raw materials is somewhat more complicated. Generally speaking, it seems to make sense for resource-rich, underdeveloped countries to export raw materials and get them back in the form of processed capital goods, such as tractors, to develop their agricultural sector, which should eventually make them more self-sufficient. But there is a catch here. For specialization to be mutually beneficial, the products have to be traded at constant cost ratios (the terms of trade have to remain relatively constant). If they don't, the smaller country—now totally dependent on income from the exportation of a primary product—is also totally dependent on world prices remaining constant, which they almost never do.

Recently in the Philippines there was a rather dramatic example.

> Sugarcane was first produced on the archipelago as a snack food. Not until the mid-1800s did the colony's Spanish rulers decide to explore the possibilities of large-scale sugar production for export.
>
> The island of Negros, which had an ideal environment for sugar production, was converted into a monocrop [single crop] zone. By the late 1800s, half of the nation's sugar was being harvested in Negros. In the years of U.S. colonial rule, the United States encouraged the sugar industry by enacting a series of tariffs and import quotas that gave Philippine sugar a competitive advantage over sugar from other countries. When the United States cut off trade with Cuba, the U.S. government increased the quotas for the Philippines. The new quotas increased the country's dependence on U.S. markets and propelled further increases in sugar production at the expense of diversification. Land that had produced food was increasingly used to produce sugar.
>
> The fate of Negros became tied to the ups and downs of world sugar prices. In the spring of 1985, a 40 percent drop in the expected sugar harvest, combined with historical lows in the world price of sugar, wreaked a famine of alarming proportions on the island of Negros. Yet, according to Roberto Ortaliz, the president of the National Federation of Sugar Workers, proper use of the arable land on Negros could feed up to fifty times the total Filipino population of 55 million.[3]

There are thousands of similar examples. In recent years, the terms of trade between primary product exports from the underdeveloped countries to the more industrialized countries have deteriorated by some 30 percent. This loss of income is primarily responsible for the huge foreign debt buildup and much of the international financial crisis. As we will see in chapter 7, one of the more dramatic examples is the Mexican economy, which has been devastated by the decline in prices of oil, its primary export and comparative advantage.

It would be spurious and irresponsible to say that nations shouldn't trade because the theory of comparative advantage doesn't always work out the way Mr. Ricardo envisioned it. Nations *do* gain from trade. It's just that often some gain more than others. This is a problem with serious implications.

Effects of Protectionism

One result of self-interested nations trying to get more than their fair share of comparative advantage is protectionism, which, as we have seen, usually takes the form of tariffs and quotas. It is interesting to note that, in general, since World War II, there has been a trend toward reducing tariffs and promoting free trade. President Reagan has said, "I remember well the antitrade frenzy in the late 20s that produced the Smoot-Hawley tariffs, greasing the skids for our descent into the Great Depression and the most destructive war this world has ever seen. That's one episode I'm determined we will never repeat."[4]

Indeed, the United States has been a vocal and active participant in the General Agreement on Trade and Tariffs (GATT), which it signed in 1947, and subsequent negotiations to reduce tariffs. The United States, in fact, has one of the most open economies in the world. Most other countries have much tougher restrictions on imports. For example, Brazil charges a 200 percent tariff on imported passenger cars; France limits Japanese auto imports to 3 percent of its domestic market; Mexico allows no Japanese cars to be sold in the country; and South Korea allows no auto imports whatsoever. But, still, roughly 25 percent of the U.S. economy is protected in one way or another by tariffs and quotas.

Even though there are few good arguments in favor of protectionism, it prevails and is becoming an increasingly serious problem. In 1986, the House of Representatives, in an attempt to correct the huge U.S. trade deficit, passed a very restrictive protectionist trade bill. The bill (HR4800), among other things, requires the president to take actions that would cut the trade deficit with Japan, Taiwan, and West Germany by 10 percent annually, to impose U.S. labor standards on trading partners, and to intervene in the foreign exchange markets to keep the dollar "weak" and make the United States more competitive internationally. While this bill has not passed the Senate and, if it does, will probably be vetoed by the president, it is nonetheless indicative of the growing protectionist sentiment in Congress and around the United States.

The problem is that protectionist measures have much broader implications than simply protecting jobs and domestic industries. There are at least three larger issues involved:

1. Protection of special interest groups at the expense of the general welfare,
2. The question of retaliation neutralizing any perceived benefits, however attractive they may appear on the surface, and
3. The more serious question of the shifting patterns of trade and the simultaneous deindustrialization of the United States.

Protecting Special Interest Groups

Let's take these three issues one at a time. It is clear that protectionism does save jobs. In the United States alone, almost 3 million jobs were lost to foreign competition between 1980 and 1986. Many more were saved by tariffs and other trade restrictions. But at a very high cost to the country.

Jeff Danziger, © 1986 *Christian Science Monitor.* Reprinted with permission of Los Angeles Times Syndicate.

There are many different interpretations and estimates of the costs of protectionism. One study showed that tariffs and quotas raise the cost of imported goods by $50 million a year. Another study showed that because of trade restrictions, Americans pay twice as much for imported clothing than they would without them, and they pay $2 billion more for goods made with steel, $500 million more for books, and $104 million more for motorcycles. Moreover, in 1985, Americans paid $2,500 extra for each imported car and $1,000 extra for each domestic automobile.[5] In 1986, one textile-quota bill passed by the Congress (but vetoed by the president) would alone have cost U.S. consumers $14 billion in order to save 100,000 jobs—at a cost of $140,000 per job.[6]

So the protectionist issue is primarily one of deciding what is the appropriate price for society to pay for protecting special interest groups. Clearly, it's a complicated policy question (unless you are the one losing your job), and it's not going to go away soon.

The Question of Retaliation

A somewhat less emotional issue is retaliation, which we can least rationally analyze. Given that, as we have seen, international trade is a beggar-thy-neighbor situation where everyone "does to others as they do to you," it is not surprising that the one thing almost everyone agrees upon is that protectionism begets protectionism—tariffs and quotas almost always cause retaliation.

There are thousands of examples. A recent one is especially instructive. The United States and Canada (its largest trading partner) have agreed—in principle—that a common-market elimination of tariffs between the two countries would be mutually beneficial for both in the long run. Talks along these lines began in 1985.

But, in 1986, under pressure from northern timber interests, President Reagan imposed a tariff on the import of Canadian shingles. The United States imported around $157 million worth of shingles from Canada in 1985, a small percentage of total imports from Canada of $69 billion. Almost immediately, Canada retaliated by imposing new restrictions on U.S.-made books, computers, and semiconductors.

Because of the unexpected rapid retaliation, some senators who had sponsored the bill were forced to rethink their position. One, Senator Daniel Evans (R-Wash.) was quoted in the *Wall Street Journal* as saying, "[This is] a good case study of what can happen when nations unilaterally attempt to protect their own positions through trade restrictions. . . . It's a splendid example . . . if we're only wise enough to understand it."[7]

If trade restrictions simply result in retaliation by a nation's trading partners—as they almost always do—we are, at best, looking at a negative-sum game in which everybody loses. Total trade is reduced, prices are higher, less is produced and sold, and jobs are lost on both sides. If there is any clear-cut, logical argument against protectionism, it is the inevitable retaliation.

Shifting Patterns of International Trade and U.S. Industrial Strength

Finally, there is the question of shifting trade patterns and the effect of this—somewhat unexpected—new reality on U.S. industry. Or perhaps we should say what's left of U.S. industry.

The United States was for many years the predominant industrial power in the world. Exports of U.S. industrial products (including automobiles, capital goods, and agricultural products) fueled the expansion of the world economy in the postwar period. But, by the 1970s, a series of unexpected shocks changed all that. High oil prices, rising wages, declining productivity, and a host of other factors—to which we will return later—caused U.S. heavy industry to seek protection from increasingly efficient and aggressive foreign competition.

With the help of U.S. postwar reconstruction aid, the Japanese and Western Europeans became formidable competitors in the world market. More recently, the so-called newly industrialized countries or NICs (Brazil, South Korea, Taiwan, and others) learned that they too could produce and sell industrial products. The result has been a dramatic shift in the distribution of world economic power.

International trade has become a complicated and paradoxical issue. As the rest of the world has become more developed and industrialized, the United States has lost its once dominant position in the world economy, as we will see in chapter 5. The old theories of comparative advantage and protectionism no longer seem as logical as they once did. The patterns of trade have shifted and the United States is rapidly becoming a deindustrialized nation. Services now account for 70 percent of the U.S. gross national product. The United States has become a nation of hamburger flippers, stockbrokers, software developers, and insurance salespeople.

One result of all this is that the United States has now, for the first time since 1914, become a debtor nation. To understand the significance of that simple fact and how it relates to the present international financial crisis, we will need to take a brief excursion into the world of international finance. It is a complex, perplexing, and precarious world—a world of exchange markets, "strong" and "weak" currencies, balance of payments, debts and defaults, gold, and arbitrage. It is a world understood by only a very few people. These days even the gnomes of Zurich are perplexed.

3
The Mysterious World of International Finance

I
t is relatively easy, as we have just seen, to understand how and why nations engage in international trade, but, since barter is not generally practical, there has to be a system to pay for and account for international transactions. That means that someone has to decide (and everyone has to agree) what will be acceptable to all nations as a medium of exchange to be used as the international currency. Moreover, since every nation has its own currency, there has to be some way to determine the exchange value of each currency in terms of some standard unit of account. This is the role of international finance.

Economists are fond of pointing out that it doesn't make sense to compare a household budget to the budget of a nation. The reason is that the flows of income are not the same. Since incomes flow in and expenditures go out, households have to try to keep their flows of spending equal to their expenditures—they have to live within their means. Governments, on the other hand, don't have that problem. Since they can always raise additional income by increasing taxes or by borrowing from their own citizens, governments can (and usually do) consistently run budget deficits.

However, when we begin to look at the economy from an international perspective, everything changes. So far as international transactions are concerned, a nation's economy functions exactly like a household's. Expenditures have to roughly equal income or problems will soon follow. Internationally, budgets have to balance.

The Balance of Payments Accounts

Nations keep track of their international financial position by statistically analyzing their international expenditures and income flows. The result is known as the *balance of payments account,* which is a simple double-entry accounting system involving debits and credits—just like any household or business accounting system. Since double-entry bookkeeping requires that the debits and credits must always balance, the issue is not one of balance, because, by definition, the balance of payments accounts must always balance. Instead, the issue is one familiar to students of economics: it is a question of maintaining equilibrium.

Table 3–1 is a hypothetical, summarized version of the U.S. balance of payments accounts. In it you can see first that there are debits and credits which can happen to the accounts in any given year. Typical transactions that give rise to debits and credits are shown in table 3–2. Second, you can see that the balance of payments account in table 3–1 is divided into five categories, each of which tracks a different type of transaction.

The first two categories comprise the *current account,* which shows the value of sales of merchandise and services (imports and exports), flows of income from investments abroad, and the income payments to foreign investors. The current account data is what is generally referred to in the press because it reflects the *balance of trade,* which is simply the difference between exports and imports and is a large part of the current account. Overall balance of payments figures are often confused with balance of trade data. Actually, the trade data is a relatively small, albeit important, part of the larger balance of payments picture.

Investment income is included in the current account because it is a *flow* of annual income payments. It includes, for example, interest and dividend payments on stocks and bonds, plus profits from more direct investments, such as building factories or buying real estate.

The *capital account* measures annual additions to foreign investments and is, therefore, an addition to capital stock rather than a flow. The difference between flow and stock is a subtle but important part of understanding how the balance of payments accounting system works. In a household, budget flows

Table 3–1
Hypothetical Summary Balance of Payments for the United States
(billions of $)

	Debit (payments)	Credit (receipts)	Net
1. Goods and services	− 350	+ 220	− 130
2. Investment income	− 70	+ 90	+ 20
Current account balance	− 420	+ 310	− 110
3. Capital account	− 25	+ 125	+ 100
4. Reserve account	0	+ 8	+ 8
5. Statistical discrepancies	0	+ 2	+ 2
Total	− 445	+ 445	0

Table 3–2
Positive and Negative Effects on Balance of Payments Accounts

Positive Effects (credits)	*Negative Effects (debits)*
1. Any receipt of foreign money.	1. Any payment to a foreign country.
2. Any earning on an investment in a foreign country.	2. Any investment in a foreign country.
3. Any sale of goods or services abroad (export).	3. Any purchase of goods and services abroad (import).
4. Any gift or aid from a foreign country.	4. Any gift or aid given abroad.
5. Any foreign sale of stocks or bonds.	5. Any purchase of stocks or bonds from abroad.

are the paycheck, while stocks are the accumulated assets, either financial or real. Flows of income add to the stock if there is a surplus and they reduce it if there is a deficit.

The *reserve account* merely measures net additions to or deductions from a country's reserve assets that result from international transactions. It is, theoretically, the account that makes the others balance. Nations accumulate reserves in the form of foreign currencies (if they sell more abroad than they buy) or in gold (if they mine it or buy it), or in deposits with the International Monetary Fund, which serves as the central banks' bank.

Statistical discrepancies are included partly because the accounts must by definition balance, but, more importantly, because the balance of payments data are, at best, an exercise in statistical fantasy and are not, in fact, very accurate. (In 1984 the statistical discrepancy in the U.S. balance of payments accounts amounted to around $31 billion.) But, like most economic statistical data, they are useful not so much for the actual numbers involved but because such data allow us to discern trends that tell us a lot about how and where things are going.

Now, by looking again at table 3–1, we can understand how balance of payments accounting works and why it is so important. In this hypothetical year, in its current account, the United States exported some $220 billion worth of goods and services, and it imported $350 billion. So, obviously, it ran a balance of trade deficit of $130 billion. Since, in this householdlike world, a country can't spend more than it earns unless the difference is borrowed or comes out of savings, something has to happen to balance the deficit. (However, as we will see in the following chapter, the United States has some special spending privileges, because the U.S. dollar is the key international currency.)

Also, in its current account for that year, the United States earned more from its investments abroad ($90 billion) than foreigners earned from their U.S.

investments ($70 billion). The net difference of $20 billion paid for part of the trade deficit. The current account was, nonetheless, in deficit.

The rest of the deficit consisted of a considerable excess of net receipts from foreign investments made in the United States compared to U.S. investments made abroad ($125 billion versus $25 billion). This almost balanced the account, but not quite. A $10 billion deficit remained which had to—in essence—be paid by drawing down by $8 billion U.S. savings—accumulations of foreign currencies were spent, gold was sold, or funds were withdrawn from the U.S. "savings account" with the International Monetary Fund. The rest was covered by a $2 billion statistical discrepancy in the U.S. favor. The net balance of payments is, of course, zero, which is what it must be according to the prevailing rules of the game.

Adjustments and Equilibrium in the Balance of Payments

Now, if you were a doctor of international economics looking at a chart—table 3–1—on your patient—the U.S. economy—what would be your diagnosis? Clearly, the accounts balance, so the accountants are satisfied, but even with this sketchy data, we can see that there are some equilibrium problems, so this patient's condition won't satisfy the economists.

The country is running a huge trade deficit, covered only by a small net flow of investment income and a very large flow of new foreign investments, and it is even being forced to draw down its reserves. Is this something that can continue forever? Maybe, maybe not—it all depends on the discipline of the international financial system. On the surface, with the limited data we have, it would appear that any country that is buying more than it is selling while depending on foreign investors to make up the difference is courting problems. What happens if, for some reason, foreign investors decide the United States is not such a good place to invest after all and withdraw their investments? As you can probably imagine, economic theory has an answer to this question: Exchange rates should automatically adjust any balance of payment disequilibrium.

Every country in the world has a currency with a rate at which it exchanges for another country's currency. (Look at table 3–3 for some examples.) These rates of exchange fluctuate every day depending on economic circumstances within the two countries and transactions between them. And they affect all of us in a very direct way.

Exchange rates come to your attention a little more dramatically if you are on a vacation or a business trip in a foreign country. One day you cash a $10 traveler's check in Japan and you get, say, 2,000 yen for it, which is about enough to get you into a movie. Then, the next day, the value of the dollar

Table 3–3
Foreign Exchange Rates, August 11, 1986
(foreign currency per dollar)

New York Rates	Monday	6 Months Ago	Year Ago
Belgian franc[a]	42.53	48.81	56.60
Brazilian cruzado	14.91	N.A.	N.A.
British pound	0.67	0.71	0.72
Canadian dollar	1.38	1.39	1.35
Dutch guilder	2.31	2.68	3.13
French franc	6.68	7.28	8.52
Greek drachma	134.25	145.75	131.80
Hong Kong dollar	7.79	7.79	7.77
Irish punt	0.74	0.78	0.89
Israeli shekel	1.48	1.49	N.A.
Italian lira	1415.00	1617.50	873.00
Japanese yen	153.65	187.50	236.70
Mexican peso[b]	667.00	448.00	330.00
Norwegian krone	7.34	7.39	8.24
Spanish peseta	133.57	150.13	164.70
Swedish krona	6.92	7.50	8.31
Swiss franc	1.65	1.99	2.29
West German mark	2.05	2.37	2.78

Source: First American Bank of New York.
[a]Commercial rate.
[b]Floating rate.

falls and you get only 1,800 yen for your $10. Since prices have not changed in Japan, you have to come up with more money—in this case another dollar—if you want to see another movie. Such exchange rate fluctuations happen all the time. What causes them?

Within the country, when people make purchases of goods or services, there is only one currency involved, so the process is fairly simple. You hand over the money to someone and they sell you what you want. The price you pay is, generally speaking, determined by the supply of the product at the time and people's demand for it.

But when you buy an imported product, a much more complicated exchange process is triggered. If, for example, you buy a Japanese automobile, you pay for it in dollars, and that's all you have to think about. However, Japanese auto producers can't pay their bills in dollars; they need yen. So, somewhere along the line, your dollars have to be changed into yen so the Japanese auto producers can be paid in their own currency.

This exchange takes place in the foreign exchange market, which is why foreign money is called foreign exchange. The amount of yen that a dollar will buy depends on a number of factors, but mostly it's a matter of how many yen Americans in general are wanting compared to how many dollars the Japanese are wanting. In 1985, the United States wanted (imported) $68.8

billion worth of Japanese products, but the Japanese wanted (imported) only $22.6 billion worth of U.S. goods. So, the trade deficit with Japan was $46.2 billion.

Now, when the Japanese are selling more in the United States than the United States sells there (as has been the case since 1973, as seen in figure 3–1), Americans also are wanting more yen than they want dollars. And, because of this excess demand for yen, it would seem to follow that the price of yen is going to go up, which is another way of saying that Americans will get fewer yen per dollar, which is another way of saying that the value of the dollar will fall.

When the dollar is down against the yen, imports from Japan are costing more in the United States, but exports to Japan are costing the Japanese less. So the United States sells them more at lower prices; they sell the United States less at higher prices.

Both sides lose and gain in this process. Americans pay higher prices for the Hondas and the Sonys, but the fact that Japanese goods are becoming more expensive means that American consumers should switch to domestically produced

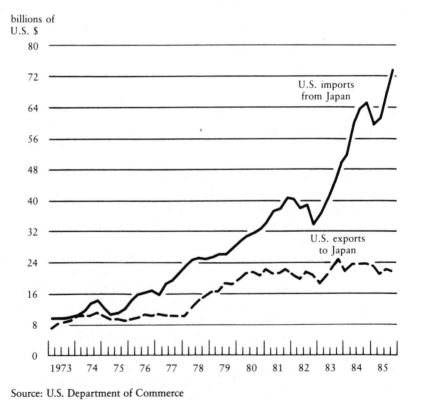

Source: U.S. Department of Commerce

Figure 3–1. U.S.–Japanese Trade Flows, 1973–85

goods and that more jobs will be created in the United States. For the Japanese, it's the opposite: lower prices for the American blue jeans and airplanes at the expense of less employment. So exchange rate fluctuations affect everybody in a very direct way.

The Determination of Exchange Rates

As we have seen, the price of one country's goods in relation to another's depends on the rate of exchange between their currencies. If rates of exchange are left to fluctuate freely according to the laws of supply and demand, then they simply reflect the reciprocal demand for goods and services. This is because the demand for foreign currencies (foreign exchange) is a *derived demand,* derived from the demand for imports and exports.

When two countries are trading, there are really two markets involved: the *product market* and the *foreign exchange market.* This complicates the process considerably. To see why, let's examine a simple case of a trade between the United States and Japan. Since there are two countries involved, the process is doubly complicated, which is one of the reasons international economics is so difficult to understand.

Of course, as we just saw, everything depends on which side of the border you're on. U.S. producers want dollars for their products, since they can't pay their bills in yen; for the same reason, Japanese exporters want yen, not dollars. So when the products are exchanged, dollars and yen must also be exchanged. This means that U.S. demand for Japanese products is also the U.S. demand for yen and, of course, vice versa. If, as is usually the case, the United States is demanding more Japanese exports (imports to Americans) than the Japanese are demanding U.S. exports (Japanese imports), then there is more demand for yen than demand for dollars; the price of yen in terms of dollars should rise accordingly. Looked at another way, the Americans are supplying more dollars than the Japanese are supplying yen, so the price of dollars, as measured in yen, should fall accordingly.

This is shown in figure 3–2. The Japanese demand for dollars is *derived* from their demand for U.S. exports, but the *supply* of dollars comes from U.S. demand for their exports. These two countervailing forces make up a market for dollars in terms of yen. Of course, to make a market for yen in terms of dollars, everything is reversed.

Assuming that exchange rates are flexible and automatically adjust according to supply and demand, they would (as shown in figure 3–3) adjust to equilibrium at the point at which 150 yen equal one dollar. At that price, exports and imports between the two countries would be equal. Neither nation would have a deficit or a surplus. This is the system in place from 1973–1985. As figure 3–4 shows, exchange rates have fluctuated considerably over the

Japanese demand for U.S. exports and demand for dollars

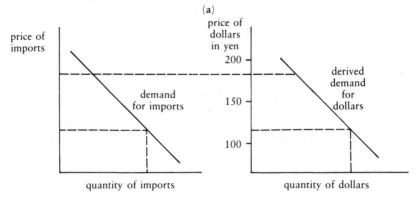

U.S. demand for Japanese exports and supply of dollars

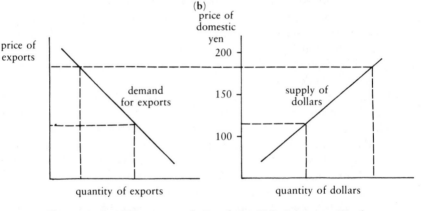

Figure 3–2. Currency and Goods in U.S.–Japanese Trade

period, but not sufficiently to bring trade into balance—for reasons to which we will return shortly. (Another way to deal with international balance of payments disequilibrium is through the gold exchange system, wherein each country's currency is pegged to a set amount of gold. This system was used for many years, but was abandoned after World War II. We will take up this point in the following chapter.)

Managed Exchange Rates

The *free-flexible exchange rate system* in place from 1973 to 1985 worked fairly well until around 1982, when the U.S. current account deficit began to grow at alarming rates, as seen in table 3–4. Concerned that things were getting out of hand, the Group of 5 industrialized countries, at the initiative of U.S. Secretary of Treasury James Baker, III, met at the Plaza Hotel in New York

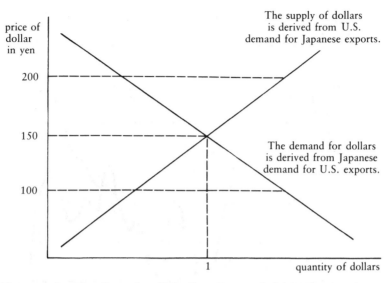

Figure 3–3. The Quantity of Dollars Demanded by Japan and Supplied by the United States

and agreed to begin (again) managing exchange rates. This agreement—the Plaza Agreement—was a momentous change in international economic policy.

Managing exchange rates simply requires participating countries to intervene in the foreign exchange markets whenever any country's balance of payments appears to be moving toward disequilibrium. In order to more clearly understand how this works, simply consider any market, for example, wheat in the commodities market. Anyone who owns enough wheat can control wheat prices by entering the market and supplying wheat any time the price of wheat begins to rise. This has the effect of stabilizing or destabilizing wheat prices, depending on the goal of the seller.

Since the foreign exchange market is simply a market for a commodity (money) and is subject to the laws of supply and demand, it can be controlled (or manipulated) by anyone who holds large amounts of currency. This process is shown in figure 3–5. At price P_x, the demand for dollars exceeds the current supply; therefore, there is a tendency for market forces to push the price even higher, toward the equilibrium price P_e. If the United States and/or its trading partners don't want that to happen (because, for example, it would make U.S. exports more expensive), they can intervene in the market and supply (sell) an amount AB of additional dollars. This has the effect of keeping the price of the dollar where it is, at P_x, which also in this case means that the dollar is undervalued (it is "weak") in terms of other currencies and that the United States would run a balance of payments surplus in the amount of A dollars represented by the distance between points A and B in figure 3–5. On the other hand, if the exchange price of dollars were P_m, then the dollar is overvalued

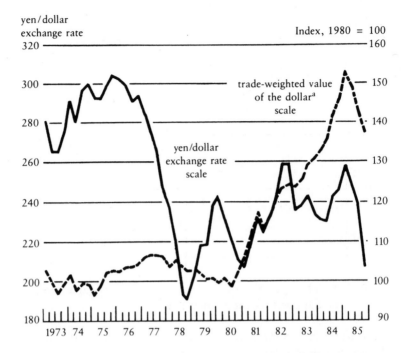

Source: International Monetary Fund, *International Financial Statistics.*
[a]Trade-weighted exchange value of the dollar vis-à-vis eleven industrial countries, excluding Japan.

Figure 3–4. The Exchange Value of the Dollar, 1973–85

and the United States would be running a balance of payments deficit (since the dollar is too strong) in the amount of *AB* in this example.

Since the objective of managing exchange rates is (theoretically) to achieve balance of payments equilibrium, the monetary authorities—under a managed system—attempt to intervene in the market and cause exchange rates to bring the system into equilibrium. Under a free-flexible system this should happen automatically.

If the world were really that simple, then trade between nations could be balanced and everyone would benefit equally from the international trade process. But, in economics, things are seldom as simple in practice as they appear in theory. Neither the free-flexible system of 1973–85 nor the attempts at managing the system since have brought about international trade equilibrium.

The Paradox of the Strong Dollar

Since 1982, the United States has been running gigantic trade deficits, and they have been increasing at a rapid rate. In 1985, the trade deficit approached $150 billion. This is, to say the least, historically unprecedented.

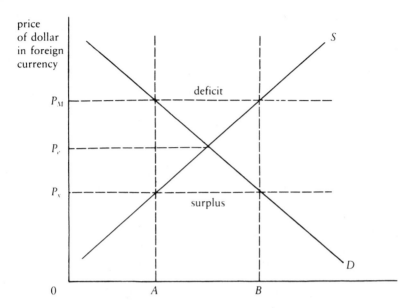

Figure 3–5. Managed Exchange Rates

Given the theoretical considerations we have just examined, it would seem that under such circumstances, the value of the dollar would *fall* and that, accordingly, U.S. exports would be cheaper, imports would be more expensive, and the trade imbalance would be corrected. But this hasn't happened. The reason it hasn't is an integral part of the present international financial crisis.

Let's look first at the data. Figure 3–6 compares the balance of trade with the value of the dollar (as weighted against a selected group of foreign currencies) and clearly shows that while the dollar has become *stronger,* the trade deficit has become larger. This, of course, is the opposite of what should—theoretically—have occurred.

Whenever a nation runs a trade deficit, there has to be a compensating flow in one or more of the other accounts to balance the accounts. That is, the difference has to be made up by earnings from foreign investments, by net flows of new investments, or by borrowing from reserves.

By looking at the U.S. balance of payments history shown in table 3–4 we can see the paradoxical events that have made the dollar strong even in the face of a large trade deficit. First of all, in the current account, income from U.S. investments abroad generally helped reduce the net effects of the merchandise deficit over the period 1979–82. (This is also shown in figure 3–7.) That income averaged around $30 billion over that period.

Also, in the capital account, large annual (incremental) increases in foreign investment in the United States, coupled with *decreases* in U.S. investment abroad, provided a huge U.S. surplus in the investment account. This annual inflow of new private investment (shown as capital inflow of private assets),

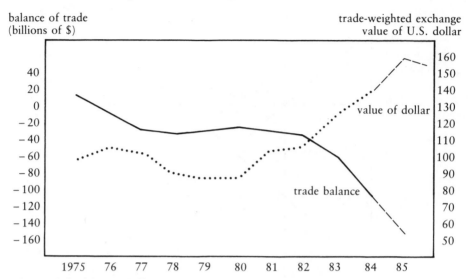

balance of trade
(billions of $)

trade-weighted exchange
value of U.S. dollar

Source: *Federal Reserve Bulletin*, various years.
Dashed lines are estimates.

Figure 3–6. The U.S. Dollar versus the Trade Deficit, 1975–85

which amounted to $125 billion in 1985, more than anything increased foreign demand for the dollar and kept it strong when, in the face of a large trade deficit, it should have been weak.

There are several reasons for this unprecedented shift in the patterns of investment. One is that foreign investors seem to feel that the U.S. economy is a safe haven for investments compared to other options. This is partly due to the sheer size of the U.S. economy and partly to the political and economic uncertainty and turmoil in much of the rest of the world.

Another reason is that the rate of inflation in the United States has been steadily declining since 1982. This means that the real rate of return (as compared to the nominal rate) on investments in the United States has remained relatively quite high. Also, especially from 1982 to 1984, interest rates in the United States were quite high compared to the rest of the world. Even as rates later fell, the *real* rate of interest (interest rate minus inflation rate) remained quite high by historical standards.

So the primary reason the U.S. dollar has remained strong is that investors have confidence in the U.S. economy. Real interest rates have remained high, since inflation is still low. Now, the question is: What does this unexpected, unprecedented, and paradoxical turn of events mean? There are three important issues here, all of which are analyzed in more detail in other chapters.

The Emerging Financial Crisis

To begin with, there is the question of the increasing fragility of the international financial system. One important result of the massive inflows of foreign

Table 3–4
U.S. Balance of Payments, 1970–84
(billions of $)

Transactions	1970	1975	1979	1980	1981	1982	1984
Current account	+ 2.3	+ 18.2	− .8	+ .5	+ 4.6	− 11.2	− 107.4
Merchandise	+ 2.6	+ 9.0	− 29.4	− 25.5	− 28.1	− 36.4	− 114.1
Investment income	+ 6.2	+ 12.8	+ 32.5	+ 29.6	+ 33.5	+ 27.3	+ 19.1
Net military	− 3.3	− .7	− 1.3	− 2.3	− 1.4	+ .2	− 1.8
Net travel	− 2.0	− 2.8	− 2.7	− 1.4	− .6	− 2.1	− 9.0
Other services, net	+ 2.2	+ 4.6	+ 5.8	+ 7.2	+ 8.1	+ 7.8	+ 9.8
Remittances, pensions	− 3.3	− 4.6	− 5.7	− 7.1	− 6.9	− 8.0	− 11.4
Capital account	− 5.4	− 23.3	− 23.0	− 23.0	− 24.7	− 25.2	+ 80.0
U.S. capital outflow							
Government assets	− 1.6	− 3.5	− 3.8	− 5.1	− 5.1	− 5.7	− 5.5
Private assets	− 10.2	− 35.4	− 56.8	− 72.8	− 100.3	− 107.3	− 11.8
U.S. capital inflow							
Official assets	+ 6.9	+ 7.0	− 14.3	+ 15.6	+ 5.4	+ 3.2	+ 3.4
Private assets	− .5	+ 8.6	+ 51.8	+ 39.3	+ 75.2	+ 84.7	+ 93.9
Balance on current and capital accounts	− 3.1	− 5.1	− 23.8	− 22.6	− 20.2	− 36.4	− 27.4
Errors and omissions	− .2	+ 5.7	+ 23.8	+ 29.6	+ 24.2	+ 41.4	+ 30.5
Official settlements U.S. official reserve assets	+ 2.5	− .8	− 1.1	− 8.2	− 5.2	− 5.0	− 3.1
Allocations of special drawing rights	+ .9	—	+ 1.1	+ 1.2	+ 1.1	—	—

Source: Adapted from data in *Federal Reserve Bulletin* and *Economic Report of the President*, 1985.
Note: Figures may not add exactly due to rounding.

investment over the past several years is that it has financed much of the U.S. *internal* deficit (the U.S. national debt). If there were a sudden loss of confidence in the U.S. economy due to, say, a Third World debt default, these funds could be withdrawn almost overnight. This would almost certainly precipitate a rapid drop in the value of the dollar and a financial panic, if not a total collapse of the U.S. economy and with it, for reasons that we will examine in the following chapter, a collapse of the international economy.

Second, the world economy now finds itself between the proverbial "rock and a hard place." Third World countries are now facing an external debt burden that approaches $1 *trillion.* If they are to have even the most remote chance of repaying it, they must be able to earn foreign exchange by exporting. This means the United States *must* continue to run a huge trade deficit; it must continue to buy the exports of the Third World. This, in turn, means that the U.S. trade deficit must continue to be financed by foreign investments from the other industrialized countries, which also means that the U.S. economy will continue to enjoy the benefits of cheap imports, a lower inflation rate, and an internal deficit financed by someone else's savings. In many ways, this is a case of being able to have your cake and eat it too, but at the price of losing the U.S.

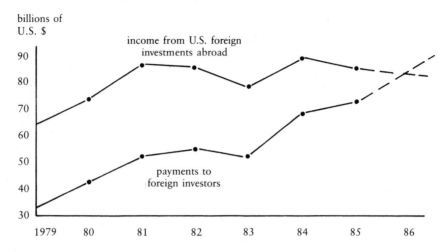

Source: *Economic Report of the President*, 1985.
Dashed lines are estimates.

Figure 3–7. U.S. Income and Outflow on Foreign Investments, 1979–86

industrial sector's dominance and the millions of jobs associated with it to foreign competition.

Finally, this dramatic and ironic shift of roles in the international economy means that the United States has already become a debtor nation for the first time since 1914. There is nothing inherently wrong with being a debtor country. Historically, *developing* countries have borrowed from more advanced countries—as the United States did during the 1800s—to finance investments in capital stock which then stimulate productivity and growth, ideally at a rate that provides a rate of return higher than the interest on the loans. If that happens, then the loans can be repaid and everyone gains. But for the most developed, richest, and most productive economy in the world to also be a debtor nation is, to put it mildly, somewhat unusual.

A nation, like a household, becomes a net debtor whenever it spends more than it earns by incurring obligations in its capital account that exceed its net income from exports and the net inflow of foreign investments. By accepting foreign investments, a nation incurs an obligation to pay a stream of income to investors over a long period of time, indefinitely in the case of direct investments. And, because of compounding, portfolio investments (such as U.S. Treasury bonds) tend to grow at an increasing rate, thus worsening the outflow of funds, as the Third World debtor countries can now testify with some clarity and, we might add, anger.

If you look back at figure 3–7, you will see that sometime in the fall of 1985 (at the point where the lines cross), the United States became a debtor nation. The outflow of payments (in current account) to foreign investors exceeds the inflow of funds from U.S. foreign investments abroad. This, in itself, would not be an event of historical significance if it were not for some disturbing longer-run trends. Even under the most optimistic conditions, estimates are that the U.S. external debt will exceed $1 *trillion* by 1990. That is half of the 1986 national debt (mostly internal) and 25 percent of the total U.S. output of goods and services in 1985.

One result of such a staggering external debt is that it will engender an estimated outflow (on current account) of some $100 billion annually in interest and dividend payments to other countries. If present trends continue, this would push the total current account deficit into the $200–300 billion range, which would, in turn, cause the external debt to double to $2 trillion by 1993.

The reason for this unsettling turn of events is that while U.S. investment abroad has declined dramatically since 1982, foreign investment in the United States has been increasing rapidly. As shown in figure 3–8, total (accumulated) U.S. foreign investment abroad exceeded foreign investments in the United States until 1984. Incrementally (on an annual basis), the annual inflow of investments made in the United States began to exceed the annual outflow in the summer of 1982. This is shown in figure 3–9. The reason that U.S. investments abroad have declined so rapidly is that investors are concerned about the fragility of the international financial system and a possible default by one of the heavily indebted Third World countries.

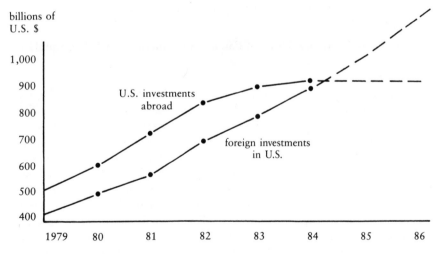

Source: *Economic Report of the President,* 1986.
Dashed lines are estimates.

Figure 3–8. Total U.S. Assets Abroad and Foreign Assets in the United States, 1979–86

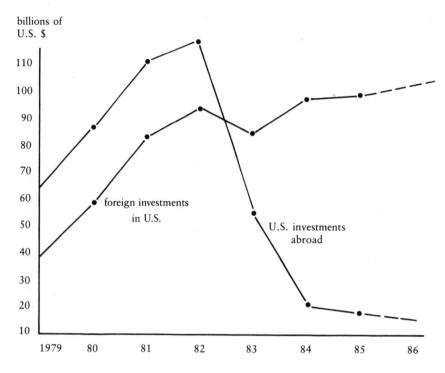

Source: *Economic Report of the President,* 1986.
Dashed lines are estimates.

Figure 3–9. Annual Flows of Foreign Investment in the U.S. Capital Account, 1979–86

Since new investments typically yield a lower rate of return in the early stages (as new factories are built, and so on), it took some time for the outflows on the new investments in the United States to exceed the inflows from the more mature U.S. investments abroad, but, as we have seen, that did begin to occur by 1985. What this means is, first, that as larger and larger shares of the U.S. internal national debt are owned by foreign interests, more and more U.S. resources will have to flow abroad to service the debt. This will mean that the benefits of cheaper imports currently enjoyed by the United States will no longer be possible. The United States will be forced into austerity programs and a general reduction of its standard of living just to pay its debts—much as the Third World countries are now being forced to do.

Moreover, it means that the United States has now exchanged roles with Japan and some of the Western European countries. As you can see by looking at figure 3–10, Japan is now the world's largest creditor nation, the United States the largest debtor. It should be clear by now that it is logically inconsistent

net foreign
assets in billions
of U.S. $

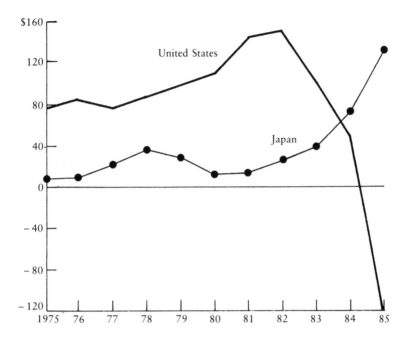

Sources: 1975–1984 data are from the U.S. Department of Commerce and Japanese
Ministry of Finance; 1985 projections come from Kemper Financial Services.

**Figure 3–10. The United States and Japan as Debtor and Creditor
Countries, 1975–85**

for one country to sustain the position of being the world's largest spender
and the world's largest debtor at the same time.

Much will depend on how the international financial community continues
to perceive the role of the United States in the world economy and, especially,
the role of the U.S. dollar as the world's key international currency. Since the
Western world decided at Bretton Woods to make the U.S. dollar the medium
of exchange for international transactions, the strength of the U.S. economy—
and the U.S. dollar—has become the paramount issue in the world economy.
The reason why this is so crucial to the world economic balance of power and
to continued international financial stability is the topic of the following chapter.

4

The Historical Evolution
of the International
Monetary System

I n order to understand the current international monetary system and its
problems, one must realize that, for practical purposes, all international
financial transactions are inextricably linked to the U.S. dollar. As the dollar
goes, so goes the international financial system.

Many people still think that the U.S. dollar is somehow related to gold.
Indeed, until 1971, that was the case. Throughout history, gold has played
a major role in the international financial system.

In the "golden days" of international trade, if a country was running a
balance of trade deficit (importing more than it was exporting), then, according to the prevailing rules of the game, some kind of financial transaction had
to occur to compensate for the difference. Historically, that was accomplished
by transferring gold reserves, from the country that was buying more than it
was selling to the country that was selling more than it was buying.

Therefore, while the gold standard was in place, the only way it was possible for a country to buy more abroad than it sold was for it to pay for the
trade deficit with gold reserves which were often literally shipped between countries to pay for trade imbalances. However, if the selling country was willing
to accept payment in the buyer's own currency, then this gold transfer was not
necessary. And therein lies a tale.

The Discipline of International Finance

In addition to facilitating and financing international trade, the international
financial system plays a disciplinary "policing" role. Within a country, monetary
and other government authorities are able to adjust monetary and fiscal policies
to the end of maximizing economic growth, maintaining full employment, and
minimizing inflation. Normally, this is done by manipulating government spending, taxes, interest rates, and the supply of money. However, when a country
engages in international trade, it must give up some of these options and sub-
mit to the discipline of international finance. This has interesting and complicated implications.

Virtually all countries engage in international trade because of the perceived and real benefits discussed in chapter 2. So most nations have no choice but to accept the discipline of international finance. If a country cannot maintain balance in its international accounts (that is, if it cannot balance import purchases with export sales), then, unless it can mine gold and sell it to pay for trade deficits, it must initiate appropriate policies to make its own economy conform to the rules of the international financial game. That is, it must make itself more competitive in international markets. Often, this is a paradoxical case of the tail wagging the dog.

Consider, for example, the common case of a country running a large balance of trade deficit. Assuming it doesn't have enough gold to pay for the difference, then its only option is to do something to increase its export sales or to decrease its import purchases. The conventional wisdom says that the way to increase exports is to put into place appropriate monetary and fiscal policies to lower its rate of inflation, thereby making its products cheaper relative to competitors'. This, in turn, should increase its export sales to the rest of the world.

However, to reduce its rate of inflation, a nation must slow down its economy by decreasing government spending, raising taxes and interest rates, and decreasing the money supply. Taken together, these policies will generally slow down economic growth and reduce the rate of inflation. But, at the same time, unemployment will increase. For most countries, this is a high (and not generally politically feasible) price to pay. In essence, they are trading off more domestic unemployment for the jobs generated by the export sector and the benefits of lower-priced imported goods. Whether or not such a trade-off makes economic sense depends on the extent to which any given economy is involved in international trade as compared to how well it can be self-sufficient utilizing its own resources.

The Special Case of the United States

Needless to say, such adjustments are not popular, especially in the underdeveloped countries, which are often highly dependent on imports and can ill afford to lower their standard of living, but these adjustments have been the reality of the international financial system for a long time. Only one country in the world is exempt from such discipline: the United States of America. Understanding why this is the case is crucial to understanding the current international financial situation.

The United States emerged from World War II not only as a military victor but as an economic victor as well. It was by far the strongest economic power in the world and had, by 1945, accumulated some $25 billion in gold reserves, almost 75 percent of the world's gold supply. This of course meant that the United States was in a very powerful position to reorganize the international financial system to serve its own best interests. Gold was clearly not up to the task of providing the necessary liquidity to finance world trade. The price of gold had been set at $35 an ounce by President Roosevelt in 1933, but the general price level had almost doubled since then, so gold was a very underpriced commodity, scarce even for commercial uses. Therefore, everyone realized that a new system was needed.

So, with the war winding down and victory apparent, the monetary authorities of the leading allied nations gathered at Bretton Woods, New Hampshire, in 1944 to work out a new international monetary arrangement. The delegation from Great Britain, headed by economist John Maynard Keynes, argued that an international central bank should be established. It would monitor trade imbalances and have the power to force deficit countries to adjust their economic policies any time deficits became out of line. But turning over the power to control domestic economic policy to an international institution was more than most countries could accept. The United States, in essence, vetoed any such plan.

Out of that meeting came one of the more dramatic historical examples of what is sometimes referred to as the Golden Rule: "Whoever has the gold makes the rules." The gold standard was replaced with the *dollar standard* and the United States was accordingly exempted from the traditional discipline of international finance.

Under the dollar standard, the United States, since it had most of the world's gold supply anyway, agreed to make the dollar "as good as gold," redeemable on demand by any central bank at the rate of $35 an ounce. This meant that the dollar became the accepted medium of exchange for international transactions. This seemingly routine event was to have far-reaching implications for the international financial system, certainly way beyond what anyone would have imagined at the time.

Since the dollar was now as good as gold, the rest of the world could, and did, use dollars instead of gold for settling international payments, for international transactions in general, and for their own reserves. The system was generally acceptable to most of the Bretton Woods participants (with the notable exception of France). Dollars were more liquid than gold, they didn't have to be stored or shipped (a very cumbersome and expensive process), and, most important, dollar deposits earn interest while gold simply gathers dust in a bank vault.

The new system did not, however, exempt anyone (except the United States) from the discipline of international finance. Instead of gold, dollars now provided that discipline. All countries' currencies were now tied to the dollar instead of gold. Only the dollar was pegged to gold, at the rate of $35 an ounce. Trade imbalances now had to be settled in U.S. dollars. The Bretton Woods conference had made the dollar the world's key currency, and the stage was set for an unprecedented series of developments, not the least of which is the present international debt crisis.

Also at the Bretton Woods conference a quasi-international bank, the International Monetary Fund (IMF), was established to monitor trade discipline and to provide temporary loans to countries with balance of payments problems. Such loans were conditional on deficit countries "getting their house in order" promptly—in other words, slowing down their inflation rate, stimulating their export sector, and/or reducing imports if they were running trade deficits. Funds for the IMF operation were provided by contributions from member nations whose voice (vote) in its operations was proportional to their contribution. The United States had the controlling vote. Thus, it was no coincidence that the headquarters of the IMF were located in Washington, D.C.

The Evolution of the Dollar Glut

The new system worked well for a number of years. So long as the United States held a large percentage of the world's gold supply, other countries were willing to accept dollars in payment for international transactions. Under such conditions, the United States could run trade deficits at will and simply pay for the difference with dollars, but in the early years of the agreement, this didn't happen because the United States was consistently running trade surpluses. (This, in fact, caused a dollar shortage, which these days is hard to imagine.)

How did we move from a dollar shortage to a dollar glut? And what does this have to do with anything anyway? Understanding the historical significance of this requires a brief look at the data.

First, you will recall from the previous chapter that balance of payments accounts must always be in balance. Or, to put it another way, total dollar expenditures abroad by the United States must equal total dollar receipts for the rest of the world. This means that if the United States is selling more abroad (exports exceed imports), then it must also provide the means to finance it. (Where else would a country get the dollars to purchase U.S. goods?)

In the years just following World War II, the United States (in the process of helping to rebuild Europe through the Marshall Plan and other aid programs) was running huge export surpluses and was at the same time providing the wherewithall to pay for them.

If we slightly rearrange and summarize the balance of payments accounts over the period, it is easy to see how this happened. Look first at table 4–1. Here we see that the U.S. ran a huge balance of trade surplus of $31.9 billion during the 1946–49 postwar period as it furnished much-needed capital goods to the war-damaged countries of Europe. But remember, balance of payments accounts must always balance. Therefore, something had to happen in the other

Table 4–1
U.S. Balance of Payments, 1946–49
(billions of $)

Export of goods and services (excluding military transfers)	$ + 67.0
Import of goods and services	− 35.1
Excess of exports	$ + 31.9
Means of financing excess exports:	
U.S. private capital (long- and short-term)	− 2.9
U.S. private remittances	− 2.5
U.S. government financing:	
Loans	− 11.7
Grants (excluding military transfers)	− 13.1
Liquidation of gold and dollar assets	− 4.8
Errors and omissions	+ 3.1
Total net financing	$ − 31.9

Source: U.S. Department of Commerce, *Survey of Current Business,* various issues.

accounts to offset this large credit item. In this case, the credits in the current account were largely balanced by debits in the capital account in the form of loans and grants made to the European countries under the Marshall Plan. If these loans had not been made, it would have been impossible to run this large surplus. During this early period, this caused no special problem with the international monetary system since the United States was easily able to make these loans. In fact, if anything, it had a positive effect on the U.S. economy.

Now let's see how the situation began to change. This is clearly shown in table 4–2. During the 1950–57 period, the United States not only financed its export surplus but overfinanced it, so that the rest of the world began to accumulate dollar balances to the tune of $8.6 billion by the end of that period. At the same time, the United States began to lose some gold as part of the dollar balances were cashed in. This was a clear indicator of trouble ahead but was not considered by most economists to be a serious problem at the time. However, as we can see in table 4–3, the situation began to change rapidly around 1958.

During the 1958–65 period, the U.S. still maintained a balance of trade surplus but at the same time continued granting loans and foreign aid and investing capital abroad. These far exceeded the trade surplus, so large dollar balances began to be accumulated by the rest of the world. This was the beginning of the so-called dollar glut which is still with us and remains one root of the international financial crisis.

Table 4–2
U.S. Balance of Payments, 1950–57
(billions of $)

Export of goods and services (excluding military transfers)	$ + 156.3
Import of goods and services	− 134.4
Excess of exports	$ + 21.9
Means of financing excess exports:	
Private capital (net)	10.8
Remittances	− 4.7
U.S. government grants and loans (net)	− 20.0
Total financing	$ − 35.5
Excess of financing over export balance	$ − 13.6
Increase in foreign U.S. balances and short-term dollar claims (net)	+ 8.6
Purchases of gold from U.S. (net)	+ 1.7
Errors and omissions (net)	+ 3.3
Total	$ + 13.6

Source: U.S. Department of Commerce.
[a]U.S. capital outflow, less long-term foreign investment in the United States.

The Rise of the Eurodollar Market

By the early 1960s, another significant event occurred which was to have far-reaching implications: the development of the so-called *Eurodollar* market. (Eurodollars are dollars deposited in any bank—not necessarily in Europe—outside the United States and kept there, denominated in dollars.) European banks, many of which are heavily involved in foreign trade transactions, found it convenient to begin accepting dollar deposits and using them in their day-to-day business. This avoided bothersome exchange transactions and earned them interest as well. Since the dollar was backed by gold, this seemed logical to everyone concerned.

There was one catch, however, which later turned out to be a catch-22—the *reserve requirement*. U.S. banks are required to maintain a percentage of their deposits as reserves. This requirement limits the extent to which they can expand their asset base by loaning out deposits and keeping only a portion of them as reserves. By controlling this reserve requirement, the Federal Reserve Bank (the U.S. central bank) can maintain some control over the U.S. money supply. An increase in the reserve requirement, for example, causes an antiinflationary contraction of the money supply and is a powerful, but not often used, monetary policy tool. But foreign banks, in general, have no such requirement, which means that Eurodollar deposits can be expanded infinitely through the

Table 4–3
U.S. Balance of Payments, 1958–65
(billions of $)

Export of goods and services (excluding military transfers)	$ + 241.1	
Import of goods and services	– 202.3	
Balance on current account		$ + 38.8
Private capital (net)[a]	– 28.1	
Remittances and pensions	– 5.5	
U.S. government grants and loans (excluding military grants)	– 23.8	
Balance on capital and unilateral transfer accounts		$ – 57.4
Deficit		$ – 18.6
Means of financing deficit:		
Changes in short-term liabilities to foreigners, gold reserves, and foreign exchange balances, and U.S. gold tranche position in IMF	+ 22.8	
Errors and omissions	– 4.2	
Total		$ + 18.6

Source: U.S. Department of Commerce, *Survey of Current Business,* various issues.
[a]U.S. capital outflow, less accumulation of foreign-owned nonliquid assets in the United States.

multiple expansion process. In addition, European banks are allowed to pay interest on very short-term deposits, while U.S. banking laws require that a deposit be held for at least thirty days before interest can be paid.

Meanwhile, the 1960s was a period of rapid expansion of U.S. multinational corporate activities all around the world. Many multinational corporations (MNCs), which routinely move large sums of surplus funds between countries, found Eurodollar deposits to be a very attractive option compared to holding their surpluses in U.S. banks. Accordingly, large sums moved into the Eurodollar market.

All this, in essence, created an entirely new money supply, based on and denominated in dollars, which did not exist before. This had two effects. One was that the U.S. banking authorities lost control of a large portion of the U.S. money supply, which severely reduced their ability to control inflation with monetary policy, one of the primary macroeconomic policy tools. And second, it further made the U.S. dollar the cornerstone of the international monetary system.

These days Eurodollar deposits amount to more than $2 *trillion* (nobody knows quite how much for sure), which is equal to the basic U.S. money supply itself. One half of the U.S. dollars in existence are outside of any kind of control whatsoever by the U.S. banking authorities, which makes it easier to understand why the entire world maintains a lively interest in the health of the U.S. economy.

The Demise of Gold

The other relevant (and unexpected) developments of the 1960s were that the United States continued to run balance of trade deficits and that its gold supply began to dwindle. Although, in theory, anyone should have been willing to accept dollars in payment for international trade transactions (given that the dollar was supposed to be as good as gold, convertible on demand), some countries (such as France) were beginning to doubt the long-term viability of a system that substituted green pieces of paper for gold.

U.S. gold reserves fell from a high of $25 billion in 1950 to $10 billion in 1970. During the same period, dollar claims against the U.S. gold supply increased from around $5 billion to $70 billion. (See figure 4–1.) Clearly, it

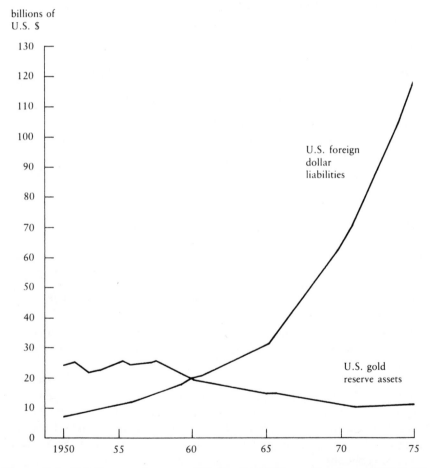

Figure 4–1. U.S. Reserve Assets and Dollar Liabilities to Foreigners, 1950–75

no longer made any sense at all to say that the dollar was convertible to gold on demand since the potential dollar claims against the U.S. gold supply were seven times larger than could be honored.

Faced with a crisis of confidence, on August 15, 1971, President Nixon cut the link between the dollar and gold. The United States would no longer honor its pledge to redeem dollars for gold. This meant that the rest of the world was left holding $70 billion which were worth only what the U.S. government said they were worth. Surprisingly, most foreign governments accepted this as an inevitable reality and continued to use dollars as reserves and as the international medium of exchange. There was no alternative. This, then, was the final step in establishing that the international financial system was a dollar system. Gold eventually became just another commodity which could be bought and sold on the commodity markets at whatever price it would bring.

By the end of 1971, the United States was experiencing a major balance of payments problem. The current account deficit was $1.4 billion and the trade deficit came to $2.2 billion. The Nixon administration responded to this situation on December 18, 1971 by signing the historic Smithsonian Agreement.

This agreement formalized the results of President Nixon's New Economic Policy (NEP), which had been announced and instituted in August 1971. The NEP, in addition to halting the convertibility of the dollar into gold, provided for a 10 percent tax on the value of all imports and the *floating* of the dollar. ("Floating" means, in effect, that the United States would neither buy nor sell currency on the foreign exchange markets, while exchange rates would be left at their own natural level or be influenced by the intervention of other governments.)

Floating the dollar and cutting its link to gold violated the established operational guidelines of the IMF. So, in essence, this agreement represented the collapse of the Bretton Woods system.

Petrodollar Recycling

By 1973, with the dollar firmly entrenched as the world's key currency, the stage was set for the beginning of what was to be the most serious crisis ever faced by the international monetary system. Interestingly, what happened was as much a political problem as an economic one.

Outraged by the U.S. support of Israel during the Yom Kippur War, OPEC placed an embargo on oil sales to the United States and, later, when that was relaxed, raised the price of oil from $1.30 a barrel in 1970 to $10.72 in 1975 and $28.67 by 1980. Since virtually all oil transactions are carried on in dollars and because, at the time, the United States was dependent on OPEC for almost 50 percent of its oil imports, this sent an inflationary shock through the United States and the rest of the world.

Having no short-run alternative, the United States and the rest of the world paid OPEC's price. The result, among other things, was one of the most massive transfers of wealth in history. Hundreds of billions of dollars were transferred to the Middle East, which was, in turn, faced with the ironic and paradoxical problem of what to do with this windfall. Clearly, their own economies couldn't absorb such an injection of funds without risking runaway inflation, so they had no alternative but to look for other places to invest them.

In spite of the problems caused by the oil shock, the U.S. economy was still the strongest in the world so the only logical thing for the dollar-rich OPEC nations to do was to cycle the oil revenues back into the United States and European banks. The details of this are shown in table 4–4. Now it was the U.S. and European banks that were faced with a paradoxical dilemma: billions in new deposits and, with a recession going on in the United States (caused in part by the higher oil prices), no where to put them to work. Since banks must pay interest on deposits, it follows that they can only survive if they can loan out those deposits at higher rates than they have to pay depositors. This elementary fact explains much of the present economic crisis.

Most Third World countries were desperate for outside development capital, especially since they too are mostly dependent on imported oil and were having to pay more than before for these imports. Therefore, they were prime candidates

Table 4–4
OPEC International Placements, 1976–83
(billions of U.S. $)

Type of Placement	1976	1977	1978	1979	1980	1981	1982	1983
U.S. bank deposits	1.9	0.4	0.8	5.1	−1.3	−2.0	4.6	0.9
Other investments	9.2	6.9	−0.4	1.9	18.4	19.8	8.1	−10.4
Eurocurrency bank deposits	11.2	16.4	6.6	33.4	43.0	3.9	−16.5	−11.9
Other bank deposits	−0.9	1.2	0	2.09	2.6	0.5	−0.4	0
Other placements[a]	21.0	20.9	18.6	19.7	37.5	40.7	18.2	11.6
Total	42.4	45.8	25.6	62.1	100.2	62.9	14.0	−9.8
Bank deposits as a percentage of total deposits	28.8	39.3	28.9	65.2	44.2	3.8	—	—

Source: For U.S. placements and other bank deposits: Bank of England *Quarterly Bulletin,* March 1985; for Eurocurrency placements: U.S. Department of the Treasury, Office of International Banking and Portfolio Investments, and Bank of England *Quarterly Bulletin,* March 1985.

[a]Other placements include those in OECD countries, international organizations, and developing countries. The last include net flows of concessional assistance, syndicated Eurocurrency credits, bond issues, and direct investment.

for loans from U.S. and European commercial banks. So, in what at the time seemed to be a logical process (capital moving to where it is needed), the underdeveloped countries were only too willing to absorb the banks' excess funds. Everybody was happy. Bankers lined up at the doors of finance ministers' offices with loan money in hand. The cycle was complete. Almost.

Now called "petrodollar recycling" (see figure 4–2), what had happened was that the Middle-Eastern countries had shipped the oil to the United States and Europe which, in turn, had sent along the dollars to pay for it to the Middle East. The OPEC countries then deposited those same dollars back in United States and European banks, which, in turn, loaned them to the capital-poor Third World countries. Unfortunately, as everyone now knows (in hindsight), there the cycle stopped, and the seeds of the present debt crisis were planted.

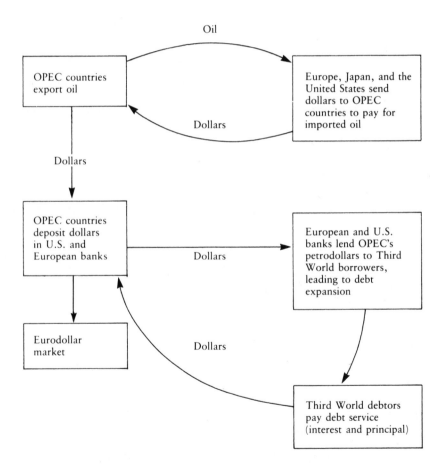

Figure 4–2. Petrodollar Recycling

The Oil Price Shock of 1973–74

The system of floating exchange rates was severely challenged by the shock of the 1973–74 OPEC oil embargo. The dramatic rise in the price of a barrel of oil (see figure 4–3) severely disrupted the international monetary system. Nevertheless, the recycling of petrodollars took place without the catastrophic disruption and disequilibrium that many experts predicted, although the tremendous flow of petrodollars to Europe helped stimulate the rapid growth and expansion of the Eurodollar market, which was to change fundamentally the character of the international monetary system.

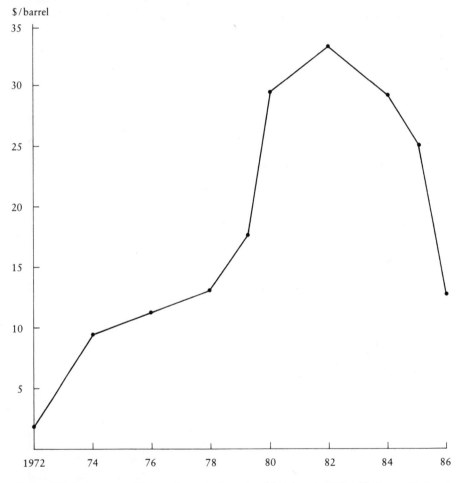

Source: U.S. Department of Energy, Energy Information Administration, *Monthly Energy Review*, July 1986.

Figure 4–3. The Price of Petroleum, 1972–86

By the middle of the 1970s, chronic balance of payments problems plagued most developing nations, particularly the non–oil-exporting nations. These balance of payments deficits placed greater and greater pressure upon the International Monetary Fund for adjustment loans and assistance, and it rapidly became clear that the IMF was increasingly being called on to perform a function far different from its original goal of assisting nations with their short-run balance of payments problems and economic stabilization policies and programs.

By the middle 1970s, these chronic balance of payment deficits reflected problems that were structural and, in many cases, long-term. Most developing nations were facing steady deterioration of their terms of trade, an outflow of capital, and the economic shocks of the first OPEC oil embargo and subsequent quadrupling of oil prices. This required new loans to pay for oil imports and adjust to declining exports caused by the U.S. recession of 1974–75. The spread of inflation and general economic instability from advanced industrial nations to the developing nations became more evident during this period than ever before.

The Flight of Capital: 1975–85

One of the more significant and persistent trends that evolved in the midst of the resulting debt explosion was the growth of *capital flight*—the transfer of money from one country to another by private individuals or firms. It has been estimated that from 1976 to 1985, over $198 billion fled the larger underdeveloped nations. This represents about 50 percent of the total money borrowed over the same period. It is estimated that about $62 billion of this money has been deposited in foreign banks and about half of this in U.S. banks. (See table 4–5.) Many experts argue that the years of continued economic austerity and declining economic growth generated conditions that actually invited capital flight. Certainly, hyperinflation and constant devaluations encouraged it.

As is illustrated in figure 4–4, capital flight has considerably increased the growth in the foreign debt of many major debtor nations. Argentina's capital flight from 1976 to 1985 represented 62 percent of its debt growth. Mexico's and Venezuela's debt growths from capital flight were 71 percent and 115 percent, respectively, for the same period.

Morgan Guaranty Trust Company's analysis of capital flight revealed that without capital flight, Mexico, for example, would have had a total foreign debt of only $12 billion in 1985 compared to its actual debt of $96 billion. (See figure 4–5.) The same study tracked the steady growth of savings deposits in the United States (due in part to the inflow of foreign deposits) and compared it to the dramatic decline of domestic savings in Mexico and Argentina.

Table 4–5
Estimated Net Capital Flight: Cumulative Flows, 1976–85
(billions of $)

	Total	1976–82	1983–85
Latin America			
Argentina	26	27	(1)
Bolivia	1	1	0
Brazil	10	3	7
Ecuador	2	1	1
Mexico	53	36	17
Uruguay	1	1	0
Venezuela	30	25	6
Other countries			
India	10	6	4
Indonesia	5	6	(1)
Korea	12	6	6
Malaysia	12	8	4
Nigeria	10	7	3
Philippines	9	7	2
South Africa	17	13	4

Source: Morgan Guaranty Trust Company.

Note: Numbers in parentheses represent capital inflows. Figures might not add due to rounding.

(See figure 4–6.) It is clear that unless something can be done to stem the outflows of capital, there is little hope of ever resolving the debt problems.

Over the twelve-year (1973–85) second stage of the debt crisis, both the IMF and the private commercial banking system were drawn into roles and responsibilities never imagined. This has fundamentally changed the character of the international financial and monetary system.

The International Monetary Fund

Of particular concern for the developing nations who were forced to go to the IMF for loans and economic assistance was the IMF's conditionality requirement.

From its inception in 1944, the primary responsibility of the International Monetary Fund was to assist nations in resolving temporary balance of payments problems. Through loans and economic policy recommendations, the IMF helped countries adjust to periods of balance of payments disequilibrium. But by the middle of the 1970s, the problems became increasingly complicated, larger in magnitude, and more interrelated. As the IMF's loan capability was dwarfed by the borrowing needs of the developing countries,

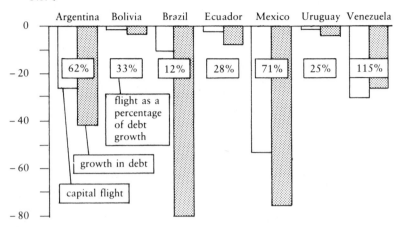

Source: Morgan Guaranty Trust Company.

Figure 4–4. How Capital Flight Adds to Latin America's Growing Debt, 1976–85

the private commercial banks stepped in to fill the void. Yet, the IMF continued to play a major role in the international monetary system, mostly now as a disciplinarian as well as a lender of last resort.

When a nation requests a loan from the IMF, a team of economic experts is sent into the country to analyze the country's economy and its balance of payments problems. Before approving a loan, the IMF generally requires that the country agree to a set of comprehensive economic policies and targeted economic goals in order to qualify for the loan. This "conditionality" requirement is felt to be necessary in order to ensure that the country will get its own economic house in order, which also signals the commercial banking community that the country is taking the kinds of measures deemed necessary to enable it to make good on its debt obligations. So, in effect, the IMF loan approval becomes a prerequisite for a debtor country to obtain more loans from private commercial banking sources.

Typically, the IMF's analysis of a country's balance of payments problems concludes that the country needs to expand its exports, reduce its imports, curb its rate of inflation, and cut its domestic deficit by decreasing the level of government spending. If the country can properly stabilize its economy, then—the argument goes—it will be easier to attract private foreign investment and reduce the flight of capital. While this analysis and strategy seem logical, there are obvious and predictable costs and consequences.

First, the IMF normally demands that a country's domestic deficit be significantly reduced. This requires a country to reduce its level of government spending, particularly for agricultural subsidies, price supports, and projects

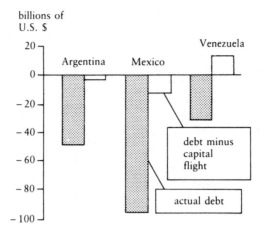

Source: Morgan Guaranty Trust Company.

Figure 4–5. The Debt Picture in Mexico, Venezuela, and Argentina if There Had Been No Capital Flight, 1985

in the public sector. Implicit in the IMF's strategy is a philosophy that views the state's role in the economy as inefficient. There is a clear bias toward free enterprise as the primary mechanism for generating economic growth and stability. But for an already underdeveloped country to cut back on its social spending and reorder its priorities means not only a reduction in its standard of living but also an increased potential for political instability.

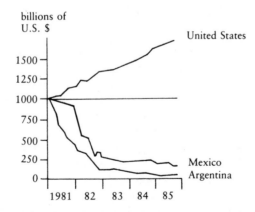

Source: Morgan Guaranty Trust Company.

Figure 4–6. Domestic Savings Deposits in the United States, Mexico, and Argentina, 1981–85

In addition to spending cuts, the IMF usually requires that a tight monetary policy be implemented to bring down excessive rates of inflation. This will decrease inflation, but usually at the short-term cost of reduced economic growth. So a contractionary fiscal policy in conjunction with a tight monetary policy normally induces a decline in economic growth.

Moreover, to improve the balance of payments disequilibrium, the IMF usually requires a nation to produce a trade surplus, by increasing exports and/or by decreasing imports. Normally, this means a planned devaluation of the country's currency. A devaluation makes the country's exports more price competitive and its imports more expensive to its citizens.

It follows in IMF logic that the earnings from increased exports could then be used to service the country's debt obligations. In extreme cases, a country is expected to significantly reduce its imports to generate the required trade surplus. While such action may create a trade surplus, it is a double-edged sword. Reducing needed imports has serious consequences for a developing nation. A country's imports of capital goods are vital for forming and maintaining the productive base of the country. That is the primary reason for a nation being involved in international trade in the first place.

The IMF assumes that a nation can achieve economic growth and stability after a temporary period of adjustment and austerity. If this program works, it will provide the environment necessary not only to attract foreign investment but also to enlist the capital resources of its own private investors. Any way one looks at them, the IMF's programs and policies have exacted a high social and economic cost from debtor nations. The continuing economic austerity from IMF-imposed policies has produced political tensions and social unrest in many nations.

The Call for a New International Economic Order

In the early 1970s, many prominent leaders of the developing nations began to argue that their countries' problems were, in fact, structural in nature and that the OPEC oil price shock merely worsened an economic crisis already in the making. This point of view was well represented at the United Nations. In April 1974, at the sixth special session of the United Nations, the General Assembly drafted and passed two related resolutions. The first called for the establishment of a New International Economic Order (NIEO). The second outlined a program of action to implement it.

On December 12, 1974, during the 29th session of the General Assembly, the call for the NIEO was reaffirmed and the Charter of Economic Rights and Duties of States was adopted. It stated, in part:

> We, the Members of the United Nations,
>
> Having convened a special session of the General Assembly to study for the first time the problems of raw materials and development, devoted to the consideration of the most important economic problems facing the world community,

Bearing in mind the spirit, purposes and principles of the Charter of the United Nations to promote the economic advancement and social progress of all people,

Solemnly proclaim our united determination to work urgently for THE ESTABLISHMENT OF A NEW INTERNATIONAL ECONOMIC ORDER based on equity, sovereign equality, interdependence, common interest and cooperation among all States, irrespective of their economic and social systems which shall correct inequalities and redress existing injustices, make it possible to eliminate the widening gap between the developed and the developing countries and ensure steadily accelerating economic and social development and peace and justice for present and future generations, and, to that end declare:

(1) The greatest and most significant achievement during the last decade has been the independence from colonial and alien domination of a large number of peoples and nations which has enabled them to become members of the community of free peoples. Technological progress has also been made in all spheres of economic activities in the last three decades, thus providing a solid potential for improving the well-being of all peoples. However, the remaining vestiges of alien and colonial domination, foreign occupation, racial discrimination, apartheid and neocolonialism in all its forms continue to be among the greatest obstacles to the full emancipation and progress of the developing countries and all the people involved.

(2) The present international economic order is in direct conflict with current developments in international political and economic relations. Since 1970, the world economy has experienced a series of grave crises which have had severe repercussions, especially on the developing countries because of their generally greater vulnerability to external economic impulses.

(3) All these changes have thrust into prominence the reality of interdependence of all the members of the world community. Current events have brought into sharp focus the realization that the interests of the developed countries and those of the developing countries can no longer be isolated from each other, that there is close interrelationship between the prosperity of the developed countries and the growth and development of the developing countries, and that the prosperity of the international community as a whole depends upon the prosperity of its constituent parts.

The well-reasoned grand design of the NIEO was predicated on a collective recognition that fundamental structural change was needed and a belief that there was the political will to implement change. This change would have required that the advanced industrial countries trade short-run concessions for their own and everyone's long-term best interests. But, economic stagnation in the advanced industrial nations, particularly the United States, and general indifference effectively prevented any serious consideration of the U.N. resolution.

Meanwhile, the system of floating exchange rates and continuous petrodollar recycling functioned during the mid-1970s in the midst of declining economic growth and spiraling inflation. This period of stagflation contributed further to the world's balance of payments problems.

For the developing nations, the continued high level of interest rates made their annual trek to the bank and the IMF that much more expensive. Their balance of payments problems were worsened by a slowdown in world trade and economic growth. Their exports and foreign exchange earnings fell.

For all developing nations, the early 1980s marked the beginning of major balance of payments problems. As table 4–6 demonstrates, after 1979, their capital account was negative every year. In 1984, it reached a low of negative $34.6 billion—a dramatic change compared to a capital account surplus of $37.5 billion in 1978. As the developing nations' capital accounts began to decline, the current account balance soon followed. The table includes OPEC nations, so one should not be surprised at the current account surplus of $31.8 billion in 1980 which followed the OPEC price increase of 1979.

As the recession became worse in the major advanced nations, the demand for petroleum decreased. This resulted in a softening of oil prices and a decreased demand for oil exports from developing nations. By 1982, in the depth of the recession, the developing nations' current account deficit reached a crushing $89.5 billion.

In addition, independent (non-OPEC) producers such as Mexico, Great Britain, and Norway began to place larger and larger supplies of petroleum on the world market. The decline in demand coupled with increased supply set into motion forces that would eventually lower the price of oil and weaken OPEC itself. Also, several OPEC nations broke ranks and produced greater amounts of petroleum than they had agreed to in order to generate desperately

Table 4–6
Current and Capital Accounts of Developing Countries, 1978–84
(billions of U.S. $)

	Current Account	Capital Account
1978	− 32.1	+ 37.5
1979	+ 10.0	+ 32.5
1980	+ 31.8	+ 15.7
1981	+ 45.5	− 6.9
1982	− 89.5	− 5.2
1983	− 59.9	− 8.1
1984	− 35.1	− 34.6

Source: World Bank, World Development Report, 1985.

needed revenues to fund large domestic spending programs and debt obligations. This decline in oil prices began in 1982, when oil was selling for $33.47 a barrel. By 1983, oil prices had fallen to $29.31 a barrel and, by 1985, $25 a barrel, before the collapse in 1986 to $12.50. This process (shown in figure 4–3) set the stage for even more serious international problems.

It is also important to note that in the 1978–83 period, *both* the developing *and* the advanced nations entered into a period of economic stagnation as shown in table 4–7. For developing nations, growth of gross domestic product (GDP) was 5.1 percent in 1978, dropped to 3 percent in 1981, and fell to an abysmal 0.5 percent by 1983. The industrial nations did not perform any better. In 1978, they were growing at an average of 4.0 percent. This fell to 1.6 percent by 1981, a negative 0.2 percent in 1982, and a still low 2.5 percent in 1983.

The Mexican Crisis of 1982

In August 1982, Mexico signaled the coming of the debt crisis by announcing that it could not meet its debt service (interest and principal) payments. As we shall see in chapter 7, Mexico was rescued from this near default, but only to find itself facing a similar situation in 1986, only worse.

Table, 4–7

Percentage Change in Gross Domestic Product of Developing Countries and Industrial Countries, 1978–85

	Developing Nations	*Industrial Nations*
1978	5.1	4.0
1979	4.5	3.3
1980	4.6	1.3
1981	3.0	1.4
1982	1.7	− 0.4
1983	0.5	2.5
1984	4.0	4.7
1985	3.2	2.8

Source: International Monetary Fund, *World Economic Outlook,* April 1986.

Note: Adjusted for inflation.

Mexico's debt crisis focused worldwide attention on an international financial problem which had been brewing for many years. But few were willing to acknowledge its magnitude until it reached the crisis stage. All of a sudden, the global debt crisis was added to the seemingly unending list of global economic problems. It suddenly became clear that not only was Mexico in trouble, but so were Argentina, Brazil, Chile, Venezuela, Peru, Nigeria, the Philippines, Turkey, Poland, Romania, and many others—most of the underdeveloped world. But the major Western countries' governments were so preoccupied with their own stagnating economies that they did not confront the wide-ranging long-run implications of the crisis.

The Reagan administration's response was to facilitate the extension of additional loans by the IMF and private commercial banks to enable the debtor countries to meet their obligations. If this meant that they would face domestic economic austerity, then, the United States argued, that would be necessary until global economic growth and the recovery of the advanced nations could improve the trading environment for developing nations.

Fortunately, some recovery occurred. By 1984, world trade had expanded at a rate of 8.5 percent and world output grew at a rate of 4.2 percent. For developing nations, 1984 brought growth rates of 4.1 percent and an increase in exports of 8.0 percent compared to 4 percent for the period 1981–82. But even with the recovery continuing through 1984 into 1985, it became obvious that the international economic problems weren't going to go away. Part of the problem, clearly, was the continued strong dollar and the free-flexible exchange rate system.

The Plaza Agreement and Tokyo Summit

At the initiative of Treasury Secretary James Baker, III, the United States invited the four other largest industrial nations (Great Britain, France, West Germany, and Japan) to New York to discuss the exchange rate problem. At this meeting at the Plaza Hotel in September 1985, the Group of Five agreed to return to an informal system of managed exchange rates.

Yet, in spite of the "Plaza Agreement," the major problems—the U.S. trade deficit and the huge Third World debt—remained and were two of the primary issues on the agenda of the Tokyo Summit in May 1986. The other issues were the pace of industrial world growth, the strength of the U.S. dollar, the possibility of policy coordination, high interest rates, and the U.S. federal budget deficit.

While overall world industrial growth was increasing, most summit participants continued to express concern over the slowing growth in the United States and Japan. The Reagan administration took the position that Japan and West Germany should stimulate their economies to speed up their economic growth rates to increase their demand for imports—U.S. exports. Japan and West Germany didn't agree.

The major issue at the Tokyo Summit was policy coordination. Since each nation's economy had started to converge (with declining interest rates, continuing real growth, and lower inflation), it was possible to begin thinking seriously about coordinating economic policies. But, since unemployment rates and trade deficits varied considerably among countries, the prospects for workable economic policy coordination appeared to be remote, and there was no formal agreement.

The summit participants did, however, acknowledge the fact that another year had gone by without a Third World debt crisis (except, of course, for the unique case of Mexico). Declining interest rates and oil prices had brought an easing of the debt problem for most developing nations. Also, the summit group endorsed a plan developed by U.S. Treasury Secretary Baker to aid debtor countries by generating an additional $29 billion in loans with nine billion dollars, from the IMF and the World Bank conditional on another $20 billion coming from the private commercial banks, the total to be spread among seventeen countries.

At the conclusion of this summit, there appeared to be a renewed spirit of cooperation and a determination to work toward a more cooperative and coordinated set of economic policies that would simultaneously promote and protect the interests of each individual nation while considering the consequences and ramifications on the group as a whole. But beyond some coordinated interest rate reductions, little has been accomplished.

It is clear, however, that the international monetary system from the Bretton Woods conference in 1944 to the Tokyo Summit of 1986 worked smoothly from 1944 to 1971—more than a quarter of a century. As we have observed, the dollar became the key international reserve currency during this period. The IMF played the important role of facilitating adjustment and stabilization for nations experiencing balance of payments problems. But President Nixon's New Economic Policy and the Smithsonian Agreement qualitatively changed the ground rules of this system. The transition from a managed exchange rate system to a free-floating system ushered in a new era in international monetary affairs.

The OPEC oil price shocks of the 1970s and the seemingly intractable stagflation of the period brought hard times upon the industrialized nations and oil-importing developing nations as well. The developing nations' ill-fated cry for a New International Economic Order fell upon deaf ears as stagnation forced the industrialized nations to focus on their own economic problems.

As the U.S. dollar declined in the late 1970s and then made a strong recovery in the early 1980s, the legacy of the Reagan administration's supply-side economics became more apparent. In the United States, inflation was harnessed and a recovery began in 1983, lasting until the middle of 1986. But this recovery did little to reduce severe unemployment, the awesome federal deficit, or the massive trade deficit. The decline in oil prices and interest rates provided some relief for all nations, but the debt burden of developing nations still remained, and the Mexican debt time bomb was still ticking.

So the history of international finance has—for the past twenty-five years—been tumultuous. Crises have been built on crises. The key factor in all this has been the role of the U.S. economy and the U.S. dollar as the international standard of value and exchange.

There are serious problems remaining—some perhaps manageable, some not. But, above all, the escalating debt problem must be resolved if the system is to return to normalcy and a collapse of the system is to be avoided. This, we shall argue in the following chapters, is crucial to everyone's well-being.

5
The U.S. Debt Crisis

While the Third World's debt problems form one of the three financial crises analyzed in this book, the other two crises center around the U.S. economy. These crises are *internal debt* (debt the U.S. government owes its own citizens due to government borrowing and budget deficits) and *external* debt, as shown by the flow of funds to and from other nations. These problems are made worse by the overall decline of the U.S. economy.

Over the past two decades, the U.S. economy has been troubled by inflation (partly caused by soaring fuel prices), budget and trade deficits, and stagnating growth in production. Moreover, the U.S. banking industry has made itself dangerously vulnerable to problems in the economies of Third World nations whose development attempts it has funded by loans. At the same time, U.S. industry—once the world's leader—has been plagued by both internal problems and foreign competition. To understand all this, let's take a look at two examples from the bulwark of U.S. industrial power: agriculture and steel.

U.S. Industry: National and International Troubles

The Decline of the U.S. Steel Industry

Since the early part of this century, the U.S. steel industry has been one of the world's most powerful oligopolies. (An *oligopoly* is an industry controlled by only a few firms. Technically, if four or fewer firms produce more than 50 percent of the product in question, the industry is considered oligopolistic. Oligopolies don't generally compete in terms of price, although competition through advertising and service to maintain market share is common. Most of U.S. heavy industry—including autos, oil, and tobacco—is organized this way.)

Operating much like a cartel, the steel industry produced what it wanted and sold at an oligopolistic price (a price set unreasonably high due to little competition). Steel cost the same anywhere in the country: the Pittsburgh price plus transportation expenses. And the industry negotiated with its union (the United Steel Workers) as an industry, not as individual firms. Steel was the classic oligopoly.

However, as many U.S. oligopolies are finding out these days, cartel-like oligopoly-controlled industrial structures can't survive under international competition. Foreign producers are under none of the traditional pressures (and tacit agreements) to avoid price competition at all costs. When there is price competition, oligopolies quickly lose their power to control their markets.

What has happened is that foreign steel producers, who are more efficient and who have much lower labor costs, are putting the once proud and powerful U.S. steel industry out of business. In 1985, the U.S. industry only produced 88 million tons of steel compared to 130 million tons in 1970. Since 1960, steel imports have increased from 5 million tons annually to 23 million tons in 1986. Imports are now 21 percent of total steel sales in the United States, and more than 50 percent if imports with much steel content—such as automobiles—are included.

In 1965, there were 600,000 steel workers in the United States. In 1986, there were only 193,000. In the past ten years, the United Steel Workers union lost two-thirds of its members. Those still working earned around $37,000 in 1986 (including fringe benefits) compared to less than $4,000 ($1.80 an hour) for a steelworker in South Korea, which, along with many of the newly industrialized countries (NICs) is becoming a major steel producer.

Also, most foreign producers have adopted the much more efficient continuous-casting method of production, which eliminates the costly ingot-making production stage and cuts costs by up to 20 percent. Only 50 percent of U.S. steel is made this way, compared to 90 percent in Japan and virtually all steel in South Korea and Brazil.

So the steel industry is in serious trouble. Is there any way out of this quagmire? We doubt it.

Some companies, such as Bethlehem Steel (the third largest domestic producer), have attempted to modernize but quickly ran up against declining prices and decreasing demand as plastics replaced steel in many applications. Bethlehem is now considered by many analysts to be a likely candidate for bankruptcy.

Others, such as U.S. Steel, have attempted to diversify to save themselves. It even adopted a new name: USX, which apparently means they can no longer describe what it is they do. Among other diversification moves, USX bought Marathon Oil and Texas Oil instead of reinvesting its profits in modernization. In 1986, it was, for the first time, listed in the *Fortune* 500 as a "petroleum refiner," since now only 33 percent of its business is steel-related. Moreover, this diversification strategy has backfired as the bottom has fallen out of the oil market, so USX is in even more trouble than before.

What seems most likely to happen soon is that as more and more steel companies seek the protection of the bankruptcy courts, they will be able to cut costs by gaining union concessions such as lowering wages and cancelling pension plan commitments. This, in turn, will enable them to lower prices and be more competitive. But that, in turn, will simply force the rest of the industry into bankruptcy. Soon the United States will have a bankrupt steel industry.

Some argue that the industry could be saved by the government increasing its funding for research and development, encouraging the development of "minimills" using cheap recycled scrap metal, more strictly enforcing antidumping laws (which stop foreign firms from selling below cost to gain a market foothold), and guaranteeing loans for plant modernization. But none of this has happened.

Agricultural Overproduction

For many years, the United States has been the breadbasket of the world. Abundant natural resources coupled with the world's highest level of agricultural technology served to permit U.S. farmers to produce vast quantities of food, far more than could be consumed. Indeed, one of the major problems facing every administration since World War II has been how to keep farmers from *overproducing*.

A myriad of government programs ranging from price supports to surplus food storage programs have done little to stem the rising tide of surplus grains and other agricultural products. One solution, which seemed logical in a world where hunger is a constant for most people, was to encourage agricultural exports. But, as one observer put it, you can't export your problems.

> Public Law 480 was enacted in 1954 to allow the government to buy up surplus crops for export. This "Food for Peace" became a pillar of U.S. foreign policy and the primary way of dealing with surplus problems. By the mid-1960s, however, surpluses had accumulated to such an extent that PL 480 exports were not sufficient to eliminate surpluses. Following the lead of PL 480, the Berg Commission of 1966, convened by President Johnson, called for restructuring agricultural production around export crops. Reduction of support prices to meet world market prices meant that farmers would be encouraged to grow more corn, wheat, soybeans, and cotton for export.
>
> The government's orientation toward export crops shows how U.S. agricultural policy was affected by changes outside the domestic economy. During the 1950s, the U.S. was the dominant economic and military power in the world. As the largest producer of agricultural products and the world's banker, the U.S. was in a very good position to take advantage of renewed economic growth abroad. These were boom years for exports of U.S. manufactured goods. Exports of agricultural products in turn helped reduce U.S. grain surpluses.
>
> This was an important role for farm exports to play, because exports relieved pressure on the farm price floor held up by government price supports. But by the beginning of the 1970s, agriculture was playing a second important role: it was the key to keeping the U.S. balance of payments deficit under control. . . .

In response to severe balance of payments deficits generated in part by the skyrocketing value of oil imports, the Nixon administration looked to agriculture to save the day. It was "Food for Crude," as farmers were encouraged to plant "fence row to fence row." Rather than address the root causes of the international trade deficit, successive administrations seized on agriculture (and other exports, such as arms and military equipment) as a quick fix. As a result, farmers were dragged into the chaos of the international trade and financial systems of the 1970s. Since then, any time the dollar rises or falls, farmers' fortunes swing the opposite direction.[1]

And indeed they have. According to the *Economic Report of the People*:

In 11 Midwestern farm states, land values dropped by an average of 17 percent from 1981 to 1984. The decline was 12 percent in 1984, the largest one-year decline since the Depression.

On January 1, 1985, 6 percent of family-sized commercial farms were technically insolvent (ratios of debts to assets were greater than 100), another 7 percent of all farms had debt/asset ratios over 70, and an additional 20 percent had debt/asset ratios between 40 and 70. In total, 33 percent of family-sized commercial farms were in severe financial stress.

Agricultural area bank failures have been running at 10 times the annual rate for the past 30 years. In 1984, agricultural banks accounted for 32 percent of the total of 78 bank failures in the United States, up from 13 percent of total failures in 1983.

Interest on farm liabilities in March 1985 was more than $21 billion, while total farm income averaged only $23 billion in 1983 and 1984.

More than 25 percent of all U.S. cropland, much of it highly productive, is eroding at rates exceeding the soil's regenerative capacity. This erosion rate is greater than 5 tons per acre.

Retail food prices rose by 24 percent from 1980 to the end of 1984. Only 3 percent of the increase went to farmers; the rest went to processors and distributors.

The share of U.S. farm products in the world markets has fallen from a peak of 62 percent in 1979–80 to an estimated 48 percent in 1984–85.

In 1980, the average export price per ton for Argentine wheat was $25 more than the U.S. export price. By March 1985, the Argentine price was about $30 less than the U.S. price.

Wharton Econometrics estimates that the cost of the high dollar to American farmers through loss of export markets was $4.42 billion between January 1983 and February 1985 for just corn, wheat, and soybean producers.[2]

There are two primary reasons for this ironic turn of events. One is that the demand for farm products is inelastic. The other reason is that as U.S. agricultural technology has been exported around the world, total world production has come to far exceed world demand.

Basic economics tells us that—other things being equal—decreases in the price of a product will cause consumers to buy more of it. This is called *price elasticity*. The important question here, however, is: How much more? And, more to the point, how will the price change affect the total income (revenues) of the firm or, to be more specific, the farm?

In a free market without government support, as production rose, the prices of agricultural products would fall, and the presumption is that farmers could sell more and increase their incomes. Not true. Why? Because the demand for agricultural products is, in general, inelastic—no matter how far food prices fall, people will only buy and eat a certain amount.

When demand is relatively inelastic, it isn't very responsive to changes in price. A given percentage increase in price will lead to a smaller percentage decrease in quantity purchased, while a given decrease in price will lead to a relatively smaller increase in volume of purchases. Since the demand for farm products *is* inelastic, the decreases in prices that would accompany removal of agricultural price supports would cause farm incomes to drop precipitously. The number of farm bankruptcies would skyrocket. The only way out is for farmers to be able to sell more abroad. But if the inelasticity problem is the rock, then this is the hard place.

Two out of every five acres of U.S. farmland are planted for export overseas. But as foreign competitors adopt advanced U.S. agricultural technologies, they are becoming more and more competitive. And in many cases, the United States is importing farm products. In fact, in some months of 1986, U.S. farm imports actually exceeded exports for the first time since the 1950s. U.S. farm exports have fallen from $44 billion in 1981 to an estimated $27 billion in 1986. If present trends continue, the United States will soon be a net importer of farm products.

This amazing and unexpected phenomenon is mostly due to government price supports which have kept U.S. farm prices higher than world market prices. One of the most dramatic examples comes from—of all places—the Soviet Union. In 1983, the Soviets agreed to annual purchases of at least 4 million metric tons each of corn and wheat. But in 1985, they bought only 2.3 million tons of wheat. Concerned, the administration put through a subsidy that allows the Soviets to buy wheat selling in the United States for $110 a ton for $85 a ton, a discount of nearly 23 percent. To date, they haven't bought any at that price because they can still get it cheaper elsewhere—from U.S. allies in Australia, Argentina, and Canada.

So, even if the government completely eliminated farm aid, price supports, loan guarantees, and subsidies of all kinds, it's not likely that the United States would become much more competitive in world markets. Why? Because there would still be overproduction, and because the demand for agricultural products is inelastic. It's ironic, to say the very least, to find that a world still plagued by famine in many areas also has too many farmers.

So, along with the steel industry, even U.S. agriculture is being devastated by the international financial crisis and changes in production capabilities. The balance of economic power is rapidly shifting. This becomes more clear if we examine the overall U.S. trade position in more detail.

The U.S. Trade Deficit

From the early 1900s until 1971, the United States maintained a trade surplus. It sold many more goods and services abroad than it bought. As shown in figure 5–1, some small current account deficits began to occur in the early 1970s, but they were mostly due to the higher cost of oil imports. Then, in 1982 (see figure 5–2), the bottom dropped out, the trade deficit plummeted, and the balance of world economic power began to shift away from the United States to Japan, Western Europe and, to a lesser extent, to the newly industrialized countries, especially Brazil, South Korea, and Taiwan. As figure 5–3 illustrates, the U.S. share of total exports between the "Big Three" (United States, West Germany, and Japan) *dropped* from 56 percent in 1980 to 46 percent in 1985, even though Japan and West Germany's shares grew rapidly.

Tables 5–1 and 5–2 illustrate the changing composition of U.S. international trade over the 1965–85 period. As late as 1975, agricultural products, industrial products, and capital goods exports far outweighed imports in these sectors. Automotive imports were roughly balanced by exports and agricultural exports were four times petroleum imports. So in the 1970s, the United States was largely trading food and industrial products for oil and raw material imports.

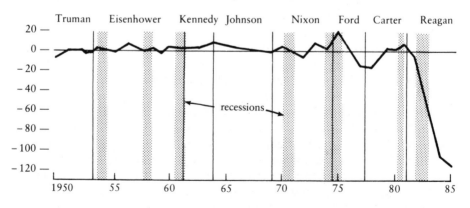

Balance on current account in seasonally adjusted billions of $.
Source: Bureau of Economic Analysis, U.S. Department of Commerce.

Figure 5–1. U.S. International Accounts, 1950–85

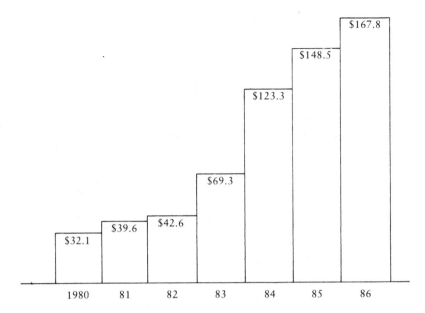

Source: U.S. Department of Commerce.
Note: Billions of $. 1986 deficit is an estimate.

Figure 5–2. The Growing U.S. Trade Deficit, 1980–86

Overall, as shown in figure 5–4, U.S. merchandise exports grew from around $115 billion in 1976 to an estimated $215 billion in 1986. But over that decade, U.S. imports grew from $124 billion to $329 billion. Put differently, 1986 imports exceeded exports by some $114 billion, or 53 percent.

Even more dramatic and relevant to this analysis is the fact that over the same decade (also shown in figure 5–4), imports from the NICs began (in 1981) to exceed exports to them. By 1985, U.S. exports to the NICs ran at a constant rate of around $60 billion, but NIC imports had grown to $93 billion, for a $33 billion deficit. It is this trend, along with the changing composition of U.S. trade in general, that is redirecting international trade.

By the early 1980s, change was rapid. Agricultural exports leveled off, petroleum imports actually declined, but industrial imports exceeded exports by 1985, capital goods imports (mostly machinery) nearly doubled between 1980 and 1985, and automotive imports more than doubled during the same five-year period. This was the end of an era. The United States became a *net importer* of industrial products, with no corresponding increase in agricultural exports to make up the difference. U.S. employment in the manufacturing sector dropped from over 21 million in 1979 to around 18 million in 1985. Roughly 3 million jobs were lost to foreign competition.

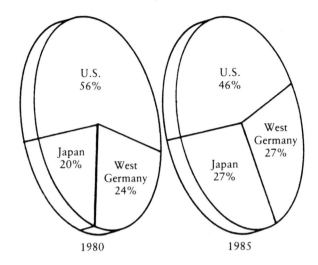

Source: Data Resources.
Note: Based on constant dollar values.

**Figure 5–3. The Major Economic Powers' Shares
of World Exports, 1980, 1985**

A key factor in this strange scenario is that much of the problem is not just a question of good, old-fashioned competition between U.S. and foreign manufacturers. Rather, it is a result of U.S. multinational corporations shifting their own production facilities abroad to take advantage of cheaper labor costs and less strict environmental protection regulations.

Now the trade deficit takes two forms. First, there are products in which the United States is simply no longer competitive: cameras, stereo components, videocassette recorders, television sets, and the like, which are almost all now produced in other countries. But the more important trend is that many intermediate products are now being produced abroad by U.S. companies and then imported to the United States, thus worsening the trade deficit crisis. This process—called *out-sourcing* or *export platforming*—is now a major part of U.S. manufacturing.

There are many examples. A *Business Week* study found that 75 percent of some IBM computers are produced abroad.[3] More obvious are finished goods, such as the Dodge Colt, which is produced in Japan by Mitsubishi and imported to the United States by Chrysler. Such goods marketed by U.S. firms accounted for some $13 billion of the $60 billion U.S. trade deficit with Japan in 1985. A U.S. Department of Commerce study concluded that imports of finished products produced abroad *by U.S. firms* accounted for $50 billion of U.S. imports in 1983.[4] That's 19 percent of total U.S. imports, or more than four times the U.S. merchandise trade deficit for that year.

Table 5–1
U.S. Merchandise Exports by Product Group, 1965–84
(billions of U.S. $)

	Total	Agricultural Products	Industrial Products	Capital Goods	Automotive Exports	Other Exports
1965	26.5	6.3	7.6	8.1	1.9	2.6
1970	42.5	7.4	12.3	14.7	3.9	4.3
1975	107.1	22.2	26.7	36.6	10.8	10.7
1980	224.3	42.2	64.9	74.2	17.5	25.4
1984	219.9	38.3	56.3	73.7	22.3	29.2

Source: U.S. Department of Commerce.
Note: Military shipments are excluded. Figures may not add exactly due to rounding.

Government Efforts to Boost the Economy

So the United States has become a debtor nation, a net importer instead of a net exporter, and primarily a producer of services rather than manufactured goods. Meanwhile, problems of inflation, unemployment, and minimal growth of GNP have challenged government economists. The government has taken highly different approaches to these woes during the administrations of Jimmy Carter and Ronald Reagan. While some problems (most notably, inflation) have improved, others remain serious.

The Carter Years: Stagflation, the Decline of the Dollar, and Soaring Oil Prices

As we saw in chapter 4, the dollar was in decline from 1977 to 1980. The Carter administration's preoccupation with fighting inflation brought about a change in monetary policy in 1979, when Paul Volcker was appointed chairman of the Federal Reserve. Volcker initiated a tight monetary policy designed to attack inflation and slowly strengthen the ailing dollar. But the economy responded poorly, as shown in table 5–3. This eventually helped Jimmy Carter lose the 1980 election and set the stage for some dramatic economic changes under the stewardship of Ronald Reagan.

During this transition in U.S. monetary policy, in 1979, OPEC took advantage of the growing demand for imported petroleum and the political context of the Iranian revolution to once again impose a major price shock on the international monetary system. The impact on the United States was especially severe due to its reliance on petroleum imports.

Back in 1973, U.S. dependence on imported petroleum had represented 34.8 percent of total U.S. petroleum consumption. Despite the 1973–74 OPEC embargo and the eventual quadrupling of oil prices, the U.S. appetite for imported oil had nevertheless grown to 46.5 percent of its petroleum demand by

Table 5–2

U.S. Merchandise Imports by Product Group, 1965–84

(billions of U.S. $)

	Total	Petroleum Products	Industrial Products	Capital Goods	Automotive Imports	Other Imports
1965	21.5	2.0	9.1	1.5	0.9	8.0
1970	39.9	2.9	12.3	4.0	5.7	15.0
1975	98.2	27.0	23.6	10.2	12.1	25.3
1980	249.8	79.3	54.0	31.2	27.9	57.4
1984	334.0	57.5	67.0	61.2	57.2	91.1

Source: U.S. Department of Commerce.

Note: Figures may not add exactly due to rounding.

1977. At this peak level of dependency, the United States was importing a total of 8.5 million barrels a day from all nations.

Even after the Carter administration implemented conservation policies, the United States was, by 1979, still importing just under 8 million barrels of petroleum daily, about half of that from OPEC. (See table 5–5.) In 1979, the United States was spending $63 billion annually on oil imports. This increased to almost $83 billion by 1980, as shown in table 5–6.

The near doubling of oil prices sent the U.S. economy into a period of stagflation from 1979 through 1981. The oil price increase brought higher interest rates, soaring inflation, declining economic growth, and increasing unemployment. But while the oil import bills of all industrialized nations increased (as did those of the oil-importing developing nations), OPEC, once again, was faced with the financial challenge of prudently allocating oil revenues for internal development, while investing the surplus in European and U.S. banks and government securities.

As a consequence of the higher oil prices and many other factors such as declining trade, spiraling inflation, compounding past loans, and rising interest rates, the oil-importing developing nations increased their demand for loans from the IMF and now, more importantly, from private commercial banks, such as banks in the United States. The IMF's limited loan capability was not sufficient to meet the avalanche of credit demand. So, the private commercial banks stepped in to meet the demand for credit. Flush with petrodollar deposits and facing limited demand for credit in their own countries (because of the prolonged recession), they were only too happy to oblige. With tight U.S. monetary policy, interest rates were at record highs, so bankers thought they were faced with the pleasant prospect of making extremely profitable loans to developing nations with little risk.

The Reagan Years: Budget Deficits, Trade Deficits, and the Strong Dollar

In January 1981, Ronald Reagan became president. The new policy prescriptions of the Reagan administration were to have far-reaching consequences for the international financial system in general and the debt crisis in particular.

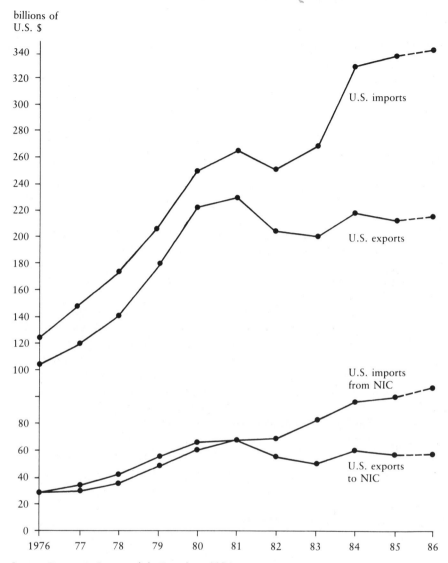

billions of
U.S. $

Source: *Economic Report of the President,* 1986.
Note: 1986 figures are estimates.

Figure 5–4. Total U.S. Merchandise Exports and Imports and Merchandise Trade with Newly Industrialized Countries (Excluding OPEC), 1976–86

Reagan had campaigned on a platform of supply-side economics. His goals were to reduce taxes and government spending, which, the theory suggested, would generate a burst of economic growth and output sufficient to reduce

Table 5–3
U.S. Economic Data, 1977–81

	Current Account (billions)	Trade Deficit (billions)	Real GNP	Inflation[a]	Unemployment	Dollar Index (1973 = 100)
1977	$ − 14.5	$ − 31.0	4.7%	6.8%	7.0%	93.1
1978	− 15.4	− 33.9	5.3	9.0	6.0	84.2
1979	− 0.9	− 27.5	2.5	13.3	5.8	83.2
1980	+ 1.8	− 25.5	− 0.2	12.3	7.1	84.8
1981	+ 6.3	− 29.9	1.9	10.2	7.5	100.8

Source: *Economic Report of the President,* February 1986.
[a]As measured by the consumer price index.

inflation, decrease unemployment, and balance the budget. In addition, Reaganomics emphasized the continuation of free-floating exchange rates and strongly supported free trade even though, as the U.S. trade deficit grew larger, the talk of protectionism had grown louder and louder during the latter years of the Carter administration.

The supply-side economic program was accompanied by a very tight monetary policy between 1981 and 1983. This policy induced the worst recession since the 1930s and finally broke the back of inflation, but only at a very high social and economic price: two years of severe unemployment, declining economic growth, coupled with historically high budget and trade deficits. (See table 5–4.)

By 1982, the economy began to recover, but, by then, the seeds of the crisis had been sown. The high interest rates of this period caused the dollar to recover and become strong once again, as foreign investment flowed in, but this was to have far-reaching implications. The strong dollar directly contributed to the U.S. trade deficit because it made U.S. exports more expensive and imports comparatively cheaper.

Table 5–4
The Reagan Economic Record, 1981–86

	Growth in Real GNP	Inflation[b]	Unemployment	Budget Deficit (billions)	Trade Deficit (billions)	Dollar Index 1973 = 100	Prime Rate
1981	1.9%	10.2%	7.5%	$ − 57.9	$ − 27.9	100.8	18.8%
1982	− 2.5	6.0	9.5	− 110.6	− 36.4	111.7	14.8
1983	3.5	3.6	9.5	− 195.4	− 67.2	117.3	10.9
1984	6.5	3.5	7.7	− 183.6	− 114.1	128.5	12.0
1985	2.3	3.6	7.1	− 212.3	− 150.0	132.0	9.9
1986[a]	1.6	3.0	7.0	− 230.0	− 170.0	(NA)	8.0

Source: *Economic Report of the President,* 1986.
[a]Estimated.
[b]Based on consumer price index.

But, while U.S. exports of manufactured goods had fallen, exports of dollars continued to be high. Banks remained only too happy to loan Third World nations funds they desperately needed to develop economically and improve their standards of living. Unfortunately, these loans brought the banks a vulnerability they hadn't anticipated.

The Vulnerability of the U.S. Banking System

What does it matter if U.S. banks are so heavily exposed to Third World debtor nations? It matters because the risks, consequences, and potential costs to the banks and the U.S. economy are of primary importance to the survival of the international financial system.

In a December 1982 presentation before the House Banking, Finance and Urban Affairs Committee, Mr. Donald Regan (then the U.S. treasury secretary, now the White House chief of staff) pointed out the disastrous consequences to the Western banking system and the global economy if there were a default by even one of the major borrowers or by a series of the smaller ones. Here is a telling excerpt from his testimony.

> The American citizen has the right to ask why he or his government need to be concerned with debt problems abroad. With high unemployment at home, why should we be assisting other countries, rather than, say, reducing taxes or increasing spending domestically? Why should he care what happens to the international financial system?
>
> One way to look at this question is to ask what the implications are for workers in Providence, Pascoag, or Woonsocket if foreign borrowers do not

Table 5–5
U.S. Dependence on Petroleum Imports, 1973–84
(thousands of barrels/day)

	Arab OPEC Nations	All OPEC Nations	All Nations
1973	914	2,991	6,025
1974	752	3,277	5,892
1975	1,382	3,599	5,846
1976	2,423	5,063	7,090
1977	3,184	6,190	8,565
1978	2,962	5,747	8,002
1979	3,054	5,633	7,985
1980	2,549	4,293	6,365
1981	1,844	3,315	5,401
1982	852	2,136	4,298
1983	630	1,843	4,312
1984	807	2,011	4,660

Source: Energy Information Administration, *Monthly Energy Review,* February 1984.

receive sufficient assistance to adjust in an orderly way. What if they are late in making interest payments to banks or can't pay principal, and loans become nonperforming or are written off as a loss?

If interest payments are more than ninety days late, the banks stop accruing them on their books; they suffer reduced profits and bear the costs of continued funding of the loan. Provisions may have to be made for loss, and as loans are actually written off, the capital of the bank is reduced.

This in turn reduces the banks' capital asset ratio, which forces banks to curtail lending to individual borrowers and lowers the overall total they can lend. The reduction in the amounts banks can lend will impact on the economy. So will the banks' reduced ability to make investments, which in everyday language includes the purchase of municipal bonds which help to finance the operations of the communities where individual Americans work and live. Reduced ability to lend could also raise interest rates.

I want to make very clear, Mr. Chairman, that we are not talking here just about the big money-center banks and the multinational corporations. Well over 1,500 U.S. banks, or more than 10 percent of the total number of U.S. banks, have loaned money to Latin America alone. They range in size from over $100 billion in assets to about $100 million. Those banks are located in virtually every state, in virtually every Congressional district, and in virtually every community of any size in the country. Those loans, among other things, financed exports, exports that resulted in jobs, housing and investment being maintained or created throughout the United States.

If the foreign borrowers are not able to service those loans, not only will U.S. banks not be able to continue lending abroad, they will have to severely curtail their lending in the United States. Let me illustrate this point as graphically as I can. A sound, well-run U.S. bank of $10 billion in assets—not all that large today—might have capital of $600 million. It is required by the regulators to maintain the ratio of at least $6 in capital to every $100 in assets. What happens if 10 percent, or $60 million of its capital, is eroded through

Table 5–6
Cost of U.S. Petroleum Imports, 1975–84
(millions of $)

1975	28,325
1976	36,384
1977	47,153
1978	44,763
1979	63,077
1980	82,924
1981	81,360
1982	65,409
1983	57,952
1984	60,980

Source: Energy Information Administration, *Monthly Energy Review,* December 1984, p. 15.

foreign loan losses? It must contract its lending by $1 billion. Now realistically, the regulators will not force it to contract immediately, but they will force it to restrict its growth until its capital can be rebuilt.

The new result in either event is 11 billion in loans that can't be made in that community—20,000 home mortgages at $50,000 each that can't be financed, or 10,000 lines of credit to local businesses at $100,000 each that can't be extended.

And of course, this reduction in lending will have negative effects on financing of exports, imports, domestic investment, and production in individual cities and states around the United States, be it in shipping, tourist facilities, farming, or manufacturing. The impact will not only be on the banks—it will negatively affect the individual as well as the economic system as a whole. Higher unemployment and a reduction in economic activity, with all they entail for city, state, and federal budgets, would be a further result. None of this is in the interest of the U.S. citizens.[5]

Many U.S. bankers shared these sentiments. In 1983, commercial bankers pulled back and began to reassess their situation. They reduced their new foreign loans and overall debt exposure even further.

The beginning of the recovery in 1983 and the decline in inflation and oil prices generated widespread economic optimism. If the major industrial nations could generate economic growth, developing nations could increase their exports and earn the necessary foreign exchange to service their debts without having to borrow large amounts of new money. The decrease in interest rates also provided some debt relief and breathing space for many nations.

From 1983 through 1985, the consensus was that most debtor nations could manage to keep up with their obligations if they would simply discipline themselves while the global recovery continued. The only perceived danger zones were the nations suffering from declining oil revenues because of declining oil prices. The drops in inflation and interest rates, and the recovery itself were felt by most to be enough for even these countries to manage their debt obligations.

But, as shown in tables 5–7 and 5–8, the U.S. money-center banks were, and still are, precariously exposed to the Third World debtor countries. In 1984, such loans to just the six most troubled debtor countries represented 179 percent of their primary capital (shareholders equity). However, this has been reduced somewhat since then. For example, the U.S. banks' exposure to Mexico alone was 33 percent in 1982 at the time of the first crisis, but, by 1986, it had been reduced to 23 percent. This, however, is still an unprecedented level of exposure to just one very financially troubled country.

By now, it should be clear that the external shocks of two OPEC oil price increases and the tight monetary policy of the United States contributed much to the evolution of the debt crisis. Bankers were willing to provide the loans, but very little has been said about their eagerness to do so. It has been documented that the banking community aggressively pursued and often pushed

Table 5–7
Exposure of Major U.S. Banks to Six Troubled Developing Countries, March 1984
(*billions of $*)

	Mexico	Brazil	Venezuela	Argentina	Philippines	Chile	Six-Country Total	Six-Country Total as a Percentage of Shareholders Equity[a]
Bank of America	$ 2.7	$ 2.5	$1.5	$0.5	$0.3	$0.3	$ 7.8	150.9%
Citicorp	2.9	4.8	1.4	1.2	1.7	0.5	12.5	206.7
Chase Manhattan	1.6	2.7	1.2	0.8	0.5	0.5	7.4	212.7
Manufacturers Hanover	1.9	2.2	1.1	1.3	0.4	0.7	7.8	268.5
Morgan Guaranty	1.2	1.8	0.5	0.8	0.3	0.3	4.9	143.3
Continental Illinois	0.7	0.5	0.4	0.4	0.1	0.3	2.4	129.9
Chemical	1.4	1.3	0.8	0.4	0.4	0.4	4.6	196.7
Bankers Trust	1.3	0.7	0.4	0.3	0.2	0.3	3.3	177.6
First Chicago	0.8	0.7	0.2	0.2	0.2	0.2	2.4	126.9
First Interstate	0.7	0.5	0.1	0.1	0.1	0.1	1.5	70.8
Security Pacific	0.5	0.5	0.1	0.2	0.1	0.1	1.6	88.8
Wells Fargo	0.6	0.5	0.3	0.1	0.1	0.1	1.7	129.8
9 money centers	14.5	17.5	7.6	5.9	4.2	3.5	53.2	179.2

Source: Becker Paribas, *Banking Industry Review*, August 1984. *The Costs of Default* by Anatole Kaletzsky, © 1985, The Twentieth Century Fund, New York.

Note: Shows cross-border risks (loans denominated in dollars). Exposures in most cases are from published company reports; some are estimates based on conversations with bank managements. (Data are as of March 31, 1984. Figures may not add exactly due to rounding.)

[a]Includes common and preferred.

Table 5-8
Exposure of U.S. Banks to Third World Debtors, June 1984

	209 Major Banks		Top 9 Banks		Next 15 Banks		Next 185 Banks	
	Billions of Dollars	Percentage of Capital	Billions of Dollars	Percentage of Capital	Billions of Dollars	Percentage of Capital	Billions of Dollars	Percentage of Capital
Mexico	25.8	30.4	14.3	41.9	5.1	33.0	6.4	18.2
Brazil	24.1	28.5	15.7	46.0	5.0	31.9	3.5	9.9
Korea	12.1	14.2	6.2	18.2	3.2	20.7	2.6	7.5
Venezuela	11.0	12.9	7.6	22.1	2.0	13.1	1.4	3.9
Argentina	8.7	10.3	5.7	16.6	1.9	12.4	1.4	3.9
Chile	6.3	7.5	3.6	10.5	1.3	8.0	1.5	4.1
Philippines	5.3	6.3	3.7	11.0	1.1	6.8	0.5	1.5
Colombia	3.3	4.0	2.3	6.9	0.6	3.3	0.5	1.4
Total	96.6	114.0	59.1	173.3	20.2	129.5	17.8	50.9
Total capital	84.7		34.1		15.6		35.0	

Source: American Express Economics based on Federal Financial Institutions Examination Council, *Country Exposure Lending Survey*, June 1984; *The Costs of Default* by Anatole Kaletsky, © 1985, The Twentieth Century Fund, New York.

these loans on developing nations in what was at times almost a frenzied pace and surrealistic atmosphere. The volume of loans generated high profits for the banks. There were promotions and raises for people who obtained and negotiated the loans. Power, prestige, and privilege all seemed to gravitate toward those involved in this dynamic process.

The excitement of making gigantic loans by coordinating the telex drew even the most reserved bankers into the debt-expansion game. In addition, the early 1980s was a period of rapid deregulation of the U.S. banking system. There was little government control over the frantic pace of aggressive lending. To verify this, in his book, *The Money Mandarins* (1986), Howard Wachtel shares the story of S.C. Gwynne, a 25-year-old with a master's degree in English and only eighteen months of banking experience. Gwynne describes his experience:

> The world of international banking is now full of aggressive, bright, but hopelessly inexperienced lenders in their mid-twenties. They travel the world like itinerant brushmen, filling loan quotas, peddling financial wares, and living high on the hog. Their bosses are often bright but hopelessly inexperienced 29–year-old vice presidents with wardrobes from Brooks Brothers, MBA's from Wharton or Stanford, and so little credit training they would have trouble with a simple retail installment loan. . . .
>
> As a domestic credit analyst, I was taught to develop reasonable asset security for all loans unless the borrower was of impeccable means and integrity. As an international loan officer, I was taught to forget about that, and instead to develop a set of rationales that would make the home office feel good about the loan, even though, technically, it was unsecured.[6]

The only apparent discipline in this era of debt expansion came from the International Monetary Fund. But that, ironically, only worsened the problem.

By the mid-1980s it was apparent that the United States had lost control of monetary discipline. One leading business magazine coined it "the Casino Society." The national debt under the Reagan administration grew more than it did under all previous presidents combined. Corporate debt exploded under a siege at leveraged buyouts financed by low-rated "junk" bonds, and consumer debt reached all-time highs.

Put all this in the larger context of the collapse of any semblance of financial viability in the lesser-developed areas of the world and it becomes obvious that an international financial crisis was well underway by 1986.

6
The Third World Debt Crisis

Anyone not living in a cave knows that the international financial system is facing a Third World debt crisis of unprecedented proportions. Third World countries now owe almost $1 trillion to the more industrialized countries. One-third of that is owed to U.S. banks. If this debt cannot be repaid, the consequences will be far-reaching and irreversible. A default by even one of the major debtors would, most likely, cause a panic, a run on the banks, and a collapse of the international financial system as we know it.

The magnitude of the numbers is staggering. As shown in figure 6–1, the foreign debt of the Third World increased from $100 billion in 1973 to over $900 billion in 1986. Between 1978 and 1986, total Third World debt doubled. The growth of long-term debt for developing nations between 1970 and 1984 was staggering. Between 1973 and 1980, the average annual increase in external debt was 21.3 percent.

The debt has now reached the point where many developing nations are having to borrow money just to cover the interest payments on their loans. For example, non–oil-exporting developing nations paid over $450 billion in interest payments on their foreign debt between 1978 and 1985. During the same period, these nations borrowed approximately $535 billion. This was happening in a period when GDP growth rates for developing nations were declining from an average of 5.5 percent from 1973 to 1980 to an average of 3 percent during 1980–85. Per capita economic growth rates (which include population growth) decreased from 3.4 percent to 0.9 percent during the same periods.

Other indicators of the severity of this crisis and its impact upon developing nations are the changes in their ratios of debt to gross national product (GNP), debt service to exports, and interest payments to GNP. For example, the ratio of debt to GNP more than doubled from 1970 to 1984, increasing from 14 percent in 1970 to 34 percent in 1984. Debt service payments represented 14.7 percent of exports in 1970, but, by 1982, represented 20.5 percent of exports. In 1970, interest payments were only 0.5 percent of GNP but grew to almost 3 percent by 1984.

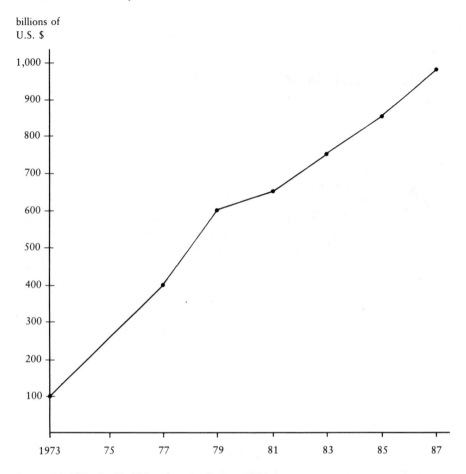

billions of
U.S. $

Source: World Bank, *World Development Report,* 1986.
Note: 1987 is an estimate.

Figure 6–1. Third World Debt, 1973–86

It should be evident by now that it is possible to parade an endless list of statistics to dramatize the point that the problem is real, it has great magnitude and scope, and it has very serious consequences for both the developing and industrialized worlds. How and, more importantly, why did this happen?

Causes and Origins of the Debt Crisis

There are many competing explanations of the origins and causes of the debt crisis. Some argue that it evolved as a result of poor economic policies and fiscal irresponsibility on the part of developing nations. Others focus on the external shocks of the 1970s as the principal cause, and still others emphasize the inherent instability of unregulated international capital markets. While everyone has their own analysis, ours is that the cause is a combination of each of these factors.

However, the fundamental problem is that the simple mechanics of the lending process demonstrate that any situation that involves a regular annual amount of borrowing and a conventional repayment schedule will soon lead to a situation where the debt servicing (the interest and the amortization) will exceed the annual amount of new loans. This process will soon lead to a reverse capital flow (a flow of capital from the capital-poor nations to the capital-rich), which, of course, is the opposite of what one would presume was the desired effect.

This process is shown in figure 6–2, which is a hypothetical example. Assume that a country obtains each year a new foreign loan of $1,000 to be repaid in equal installments over twenty years with 10 percent interest on the outstanding balance. The net result is a downward trend of net proceeds (the amount left over after paying the accumulated debt service, which gets larger and larger—due to paying interest on interest—making net proceeds get smaller and smaller). By the eighth year, the borrowing of an additional $1,000 is insufficient even to meet the obligations on the past debt, so a reverse flow of funds back to the lending country begins, unless the rate of new borrowing is increased.

A Chronology of the Debt Crisis

Stage I. OPEC and Petrodollar Recycling: 1973–78

Almost all analysts agree that the OPEC oil embargo and the consequent quadrupling of oil prices between 1973 and 1974 represents the first stage in the debt crisis. Non–oil-exporting developing nations had a current account deficit of only $11 billion in 1973. After the oil price shock, this deficit leaped to $37 billion in 1974 and $46 billion in 1975. Non–oil-exporting developing nations saw their oil costs soar from 6 percent of total spending in 1973 to 21 percent by 1981. This extra cost from the oil price increase alone added $260 billion to their total spending between 1973 and 1982. If interest on money borrowed to pay for the oil imports were added to this figure, it would be $335 billion.

As we saw in the previous chapter, this was a period of recycling of petrodollars from OPEC nations to European and U.S. financial institutions. The price increase induced a recession and generated inflationary pressures. The recession spread throughout the major Western nations and ultimately brought about a decline in demand for developing nations' exports. Unable to earn sufficient export revenues and facing escalating oil bills, the non–oil-exporting developing nations had to go to the IMF and commercial banks to borrow money in

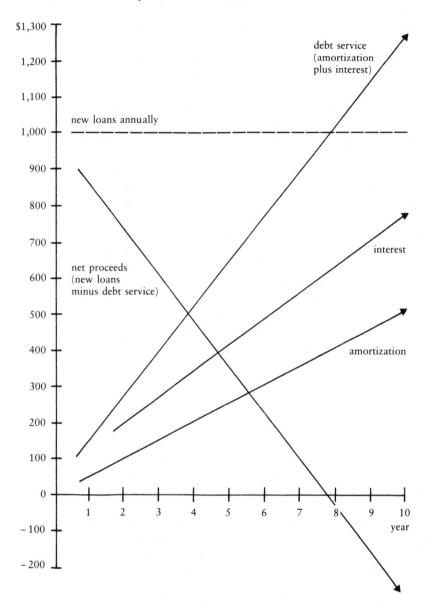

Net capital flow if $1,000 is borrowed each year at 10% interest for twenty years.
Source: *Monthly Review*, April 1985.

Figure 6–2. The Debt Trap

order to settle their deteriorating balance of payments position. Given the overall demand for credit, they were indeed fortunate that the *real interest rate* was low or negative for much of the 1970s. (The real interest rate is the difference between the nominal interest rate and the rate of inflation. If you borrow money at a 15 percent annual interest rate, but the inflation rate is 5 percent per year, the real interest rate that you pay is 15 percent minus 5 percent, or 10 percent.)

The historic chronic balance of payments problem of developing nations was now compounded by an emerging layer of foreign debt. This, in turn, placed greater and greater pressure upon the IMF and later the private commercial banks to provide the additional loans necessary for them to service their debt and resolve their continuing balance of payments difficulties.

*Stage II. OPEC's Price Increase and
U.S. Monetary Policy: 1979–82*

The second stage of the debt crisis began in 1979, when OPEC doubled oil prices and President Carter appointed Paul Volcker as chairman of the Federal Reserve Bank. These two seemingly unrelated events were to trigger a major expansion of the debt crisis.

Along with this second major OPEC price increase came another phase of petrodollar recycling. By 1979, OPEC petrodollar deposits totalled $62 billion. They increased to $100 billion in 1980. The commercial banks, once again flush with petrodollars, were now able—and quite willing—to make even more sizable and very profitable loans to developing nations. The private commercial banks made loans to non–oil-exporting developing nations to help them pay for their oil imports. At the same time, they made sizable loans to oil-exporting developing nations, such as Mexico, so that they could more rapidly develop their petroleum sectors and diversify their economies.

But the timing of the OPEC price increase, the second stage of recycling of petrodollars, and the need for most new loans to come from private commercial banks in lieu of the IMF (which was by then short on capital) placed the borrowing nations in an even more precarious position. The reasons are complex.

As can be seen in table 6–1, for the United States, 1979 was a year of sluggish economic growth (only 2.5 percent) and high inflation (13.3 percent). Federal Reserve Chairman Volcker's strategy for fighting inflation was to maintain a tight monetary policy as long as was necessary to bring inflation down. This is observable in the movements of key monetary indicators for the period 1979–82 in table 6–1. The U.S. money supply was reduced dramatically and interest rates increased to record highs. By 1983, this policy worked; it reduced inflation from 1979's horrendous 13.3 percent level to 3.6 percent. However,

Table 6–1
U.S. Economic Data, 1973–85

	Real GNP[a]	Unemployment	Inflation[b]	Budget Deficit (billions)	Trade Balance (billions)	Dollar Index[c]	Change in M1[d]	Average Prime Rate	Average Discount Rate	Average Federal Funds Rate
1973	5.2%	4.9%	8.8%	$ −14.8	$ +.9	98.8	5.5%	8.0%	6.4%	8.7%
1974	−0.5	5.6	12.2	−4.6	−5.5	99.2	5.4	10.8	7.8	10.5
1975	−1.3	8.5	7.0	−45.1	+8.9	93.9	4.9	7.8	6.3	5.8
1976	4.9	7.7	4.8	−66.4	−9.4	97.3	6.6	6.8	5.5	5.0
1977	4.7	7.0	6.8	−44.9	−31.1	93.1	8.1	6.8	5.5	5.5
1978	5.3	6.0	9.0	−48.8	−34.0	84.2	8.3	9.0	7.5	7.9
1979	2.5	5.8	13.3	−27.6	−27.5	83.2	7.2	12.6	10.3	11.2
1980	−0.2	7.1	12.3	−59.5	−25.5	84.8	6.6	15.2	11.8	13.4
1981	1.9	7.5	10.2	−57.9	−27.9	100.8	6.5	18.8	13.4	16.4
1982	−2.5	9.5	6.0	−110.6	−36.4	111.7	8.8	14.8	11.0	12.3
1983	3.5	9.5	3.6	−195.4	−67.2	117.3	9.8	10.8	8.5	9.0
1984	6.5	7.7	3.5	−183.6	−114.1	128.5	5.8	12.0	8.8	10.2
1985	2.3	7.1	3.6	−212.3	−150.0	132.0	11.9	9.9	7.7	8.1

Source: *Economic Report of the President*, February 1986.

[a]Change in gross national product based on 1982 dollars.

[b]Measured by increases in the consumer price index.

[c]Trade-weighted index for the value of the U.S. dollar (1973 = 100).

[d]Basic money supply (M1) includes coins, currency, and demand deposits.

this success came at the expense of a deep recession which resulted in unemployment rates which averaged 9.5 percent in both 1982 and 1983. As a consequence of contractionary monetary policy, interest rates soared. The prime rate hit 18.8 percent in 1981. Since these high interest rates came at a time when inflation was beginning to abate, one result was higher real interest rates for borrowers. This was good news for bankers because their real earnings were now higher, but it was the beginning of the end for the debtor nations. The higher interest rates drove the value of the dollar higher. The stronger dollar made it more difficult for the indebted developing nations to service their debt burdens since they now needed even larger revenues from export earnings to pay their predominantly dollar-denominated debts.

For the United States, the strong dollar was a mixed blessing. On one hand, it stimulated the purchase of imports and made U.S. exports less competitive and drove up the already large trade deficit shown in table 6–1. But the higher interest rates attracted foreign investment capital to the United States. Facing rapidly growing annual budget deficits and a soaring public debt, U.S. fiscal authorities were pleased that foreign capital was flowing to the country and helping to finance its increasing internal deficits. Little did anyone realize that the United States was, even then, on the way to becoming the largest debtor nation in the world.

Thus, the 1979–82 period was characterized by increasing oil prices, increasing real interest rates, a strong dollar, and a declining demand for exports from the Third World. Each of these factors contributed to the debt expansion in this stage of the evolution of the crisis.

In retrospect, it is now clear that tight antiinflationary U.S. monetary policy worsened the debt-expansion cycle. Also notable was the emergence of private commercial banks as the primary source of international lending. One result of this was more borrowing of short-term money at variable interest rates. (The interest rate most commonly used for international loans is the London interbank offered rate, or LIBOR, which varies daily. Most international loans are made at 7/8 of a percentage point above the LIBOR rate.)

Table 6–2 shows that private debt as a percentage of total debt increased from 50.9 percent in 1970 to 64.6 percent in 1982 and that the debt service ratio (export earnings as a percentage of interest and principal payments in a given year) increased from 14.7 percent in 1970 to 20.5 percent in 1982. The major factor here is the changing role of private banks. Their large-scale involvement in meeting the credit needs of Third World nations has now placed them in a new and unexpectedly vulnerable position in the international monetary system. But, it was not until Mexico's near economic collapse in 1982 that the Western governments and bankers realized that there was in fact a large-scale debt crisis that transcended the case of Mexico to include numerous other Third World nations.

As we will discuss in the next chapter, Mexico was rescued from the 1982 crisis. This rescue effort—along with the accumulated experience of rescheduling

Table 6–2
Debt Indicators for Developing Countries, 1970–84
(percentages)

	1970	1974	1976	1978	1980	1981	1982	1983	1984
Ratio of debt to GNP	14.1	15.4	18.1	21.0	20.9	22.4	26.3	31.3	33.8
Ratio of debt to exports	108.9	80.0	100.2	113.1	89.8	96.8	115.0	130.8	135.4
Debt service ratio	14.7	11.8	13.6	18.4	16.0	17.6	20.5	19.0	19.7
Ratio of interest service to GNP	0.5	0.8	0.8	1.1	1.6	1.9	2.3	2.3	2.8
Private debt as a percentage of total debt	50.9	56.5	59.0	61.5	62.9	64.1	64.6	65.8	65.0

Source: World Bank, *World Development Report*, 1985.
Note: Interest and debt service for 1970–83 are actual (not contractual) service paid during the period. Interest and debt service for 1984 are projections of contractual obligations due based on commitments received through the end of 1983 and take into account reschedulings through the end of 1984.

debt—gave governments and bankers valuable on-the-job training. It was also a signal to the international financial community that everybody needed to reassess their roles and positions in the debt game. After 1982, the banks reduced the rate of new loans and improved their capital position by reducing their *loan exposure abroad* (loans to other nations as a percentage of primary capital or its equity held by shareholders). This was wise since the percentage of potentially nonperforming loans increases in comparison to a bank's capital, the bank becomes increasingly vulnerable should the debt not be repaid in full or repudiated, that is, not paid at all. Recall, for example, our discussion of the vulnerability of the U.S. banking system in chapter 5.

Stage III. Economic Recovery and the
Calm before the Storm: 1983–86

From 1983 to 1986, there was some feeling that the situation was improving. Such debtor countries as Argentina and Brazil had successfully instituted new growth-oriented economic programs and were beginning to meet some of their debt obligations.

Both Argentina and Brazil's new programs were unique. Each nation created a new currency (in Argentina the *austral* and in Brazil the *cruzado*) and utilized wage and price controls to harness their rapid rates of inflation and more evenly distribute the costs and consequences of ecomomic adjustment. In addition, the decline in interest rates and oil prices eased the pressures on each nation as did the global economic recovery. Both nations' export sectors boomed as did their economic growth rates.

Most notable was Brazil under the democratic leadership of President Jose Sarney. It registered real GNP growth rates of 8.4 percent in 1985 and an estimated 7 percent for 1986 and in 1985, it generated a trade surplus of $13 billion, while reducing its inflation rate from 225 percent in 1985 to just 80 percent in 1986. Yet, in spite of this incredible turnaround of the economy, most experts note that the Brazilian export machine is plagued with inequality and uneven development. The tremendous growth is not filtering down to the majority of the population, and political unrest is growing.

The Impact of the Debt Crisis

The debt crisis has brought many changes to the international monetary system. But the most critical effect of all has been the historic transfer of resources *from* debt-plagued developing nations *to* the advanced industrial nations. For the process of genuine economic development to occur, it is necessary for a developing nation to have capital resources for investment. If a country does not have sufficient domestic savings and investment, it is necessary to fill this gap if progress is to occur. Historically, this has been achieved through grants, aid, loans, and direct private foreign investment from multinational firms. But loans must be repaid and foreign investment will earn a profit. Eventually, as we described at the beginning of this chapter, this will create a capital *outflow* as a direct function of the development process.

What is crucial is that a nation wisely uses its external capital inflows to productively develop its economy. In order to progress, a developing country must generate sufficient growth to pay for the costs of capital resources *and* have enough economic surplus left to reinvest in its domestic economy and provide for the social and economic needs of its population.

If the vast majority of its economic surplus is used to service loans and pay profits to foreign capital, then there will be little left for domestic uses. As we have seen, the chronic balance of payments problem worsened by the debt crisis has placed an incredible squeeze on most developing nations' scarce resources. As larger proportions of these resources are used for debt service, their internal development needs are neglected at high political costs.

In the 1980s, we have reached a historic transition with respect to the process, direction, and magnitude of capital resource transfers from developing to advanced nations. The long-run economic and political impacts of this transition are yet to be felt.

The Resource Transfer Flow

This trend of transferring resources has been analyzed in detail by Harold Lever and Christopher Huhne in a recent book *Debt and Danger* (1986) and elsewhere. They determined that while there was a small net flow of capital from industrial countries to the developing countries up until 1983, the trend reversed in 1984, when $22.5 billion flowed *back* to the more developed nations. (See table 6–3 and figures 6–3 and 6–4.)

Table 6–3
The Resource Flow to and from Debtor Countries, 1978–86
(billions of $)

	1978	1979	1980	1981	1982	1983	1984	1985[b]	1986[b]
Indebted Developing Countries									
Current account deficit	56.8	61.7	77.0	112.6	102.9	59.4	37.9	38.2	36.7
Net investment income including interest	−14.7	−21.1	−30.3	−44.2	−56.5	−56.9	−60.4	−61.4	−60.0
Resource flow	42.1	40.6	46.7	68.4	46.4	2.5	−22.5	−23.2	−23.3
Resource flow as a percentage of exports of goods and services	14.0%	10.3%	9.1%	12.8%	9.2%	0.5%	−4.1%	−4.0%	−3.7%
Major Borrowers[a]									
Current account deficit	18.4	22.3	26.5	35.7	39.8	10.9	1.5	4.0	3.0
Net investment income including interest	−8.3	−12.1	−18.0	−26.1	−34.2	−33.4	−36.0	−35.7	−33.4
Resource flow	10.1	10.2	8.5	9.6	5.6	−22.5	−34.5	−31.7	−30.4
Resource flow as a percentage of exports of goods and services	12.9%	10.1%	6.3%	6.2%	4.0%	−16.3%	−22.7%	−19.5%	−17.3%

Source: Derived from IMF, *World Economic Outlook*, table 36 and table 34; Lever and Huhne, *Debt and Danger*, table 3.
Note: Minus signs indicate a resource flow from the debtor countries.
[a] Argentina, Indonesia, Mexico, Venezuela, Brazil, South Korea, Philippines.
[b] IMF projections.

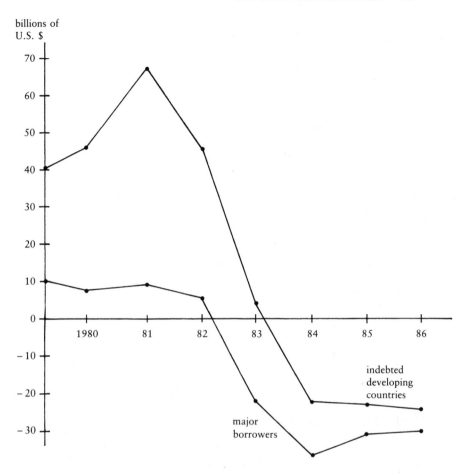

Source: 1979–84 data are derived from Lever and Huhne, *Debt and Danger*, table 3; 1985–86 projections come from International Monetary Fund.

Figure 6–3. The Resource Flow to and from Indebted Developing Countries, 1979–86

From table 6–3, we can see that the resource flow (new lending minus interest) for all indebted developing nations went from a positive $68.4 billion in 1981, to $2.5 billion in 1983, to a *negative* $22.5 billion in 1984. This was followed by a negative resource flow of $23.2 billion in 1984 and $23.3 billion in 1986. This negative resource flow alone was 4.1 percent of indebted developing countries' exports in 1984.

Looking at the data for the seven major borrowers, we can see that their negative resource flow in 1983 swelled to a level of $34.5 billion in 1984 and is projected to remain above $30 billion a year for 1985–86. In 1984, this negative

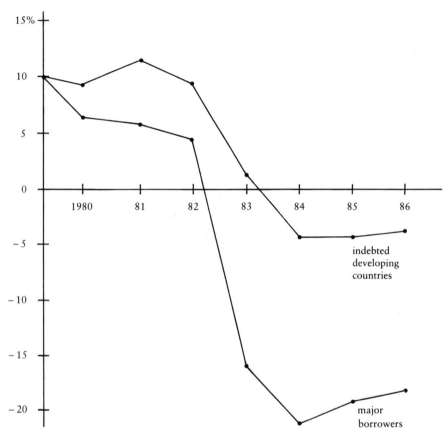

Source: 1979–84 data are derived from Lever and Huhne, *Debt and Danger*, table 3; 1985–86 projections come from International Monetary Fund.

Figure 6–4. Resource Flow as a Percentage of Exports of Goods and Services, 1979–86

resource flow was equal to 22.7 percent of the major borrowers' exports. The IMF projects that the resource flows will be much higher for the 1986–90 period.

For Latin America alone, the data is even more revealing. Between 1981 and 1984, Latin America experienced a *decrease* in per capita income of 8.9 percent. Latin American imports fell by 27 percent in 1983, while exports increased only 8.6 percent. Yet, by the end of 1983, Latin American external public debt had grown to $257 billion. From 1975 to 1983, Latin America paid over $90 billion in interest on its public debt. Of this, Mexico alone paid over $30 billion. The nature and character of this negative resource flow raises some fundamental questions about the prospects for genuine development for debtor nations and the future of the international financial system.

Table 6-4
Net Debt Transfer, 1982-90
(billions of $)

	1982	1983	1984	1985	1986	1988	1990
123 Indebted Developing Countries							
Total debt	747.0	790.7	827.7	865.3	896.5	986.2	1,089.9
Debt service	123.9	111.1	123.1	134.5	139.4	199.2	207.5
Interest (A)	72.3	67.4	71.0	74.0	72.5	83.5	87.0
Net new borrowing (B)	86.5	43.7	37.0	37.6	31.2	45.9	53.0
Transfer (B − A)	14.2	−23.7	−34.0	−36.4	−41.3	−37.6	−34.0
Vulnerability ratio (A/B)	0.8	1.5	1.9	2.0	2.3	1.8	1.6
Transfer as a percentage of exports	2.8%	−4.7%	−6.2%	−6.2%	−6.5%	−4.7%	−3.4%
7 Major Borrowers[a]							
Total debt	336.4	351.0	360.2	369.3	377.4	385.1	374.3
Debt service	61.8	49.3	53.5	57.3	59.5	87.0	82.0
Interest (A)	38.9	35.7	37.9	38.3	36.3	37.3	34.5
Net new borrowing (B)	46.2	14.6	9.2	9.1	8.1	3.9	−5.4
Transfer (B − A)	7.3	−21.1	−28.7	−29.2	+28.2	−33.4	−39.9
Vulnerability ratio (A/B)	0.8	2.4	4.1	4.2	4.5	9.6	—[b]
Transfer as a percentage of exports	5.2%	−15.3%	−18.8%	−17.9%	−16.0%	−15.5%	−16.0%

Source: Authors' calculations derived from IMF, *World Economic Outlook*, April 1985; Lever and Huhne, *Debt and Danger*, table 4.
[a]Argentina, Brazil, Indonesia, South Korea, Mexico, Philippines, and Venezuela (which together accounted for 44 percent of LDC debt in1984).
[b]Theoretically infinite.

What We Can Expect in the Future

Using the IMF projections, Lever and Huhne also examined the data for *net debt transfer* (the balance between the interest and repayment of old debt paid out and the new money received from banks). This is shown in table 6–4 and figures 6–5 and 6–6. The IMF's projection for 1990 is for the net debt transfer to increase to a level of $39.9 billion or 16 percent of exports. What is disturbing about this projection is that the largest transfers are *still to come* and they will continue to grow even under the most favorable IMF assumptions about future economic growth.

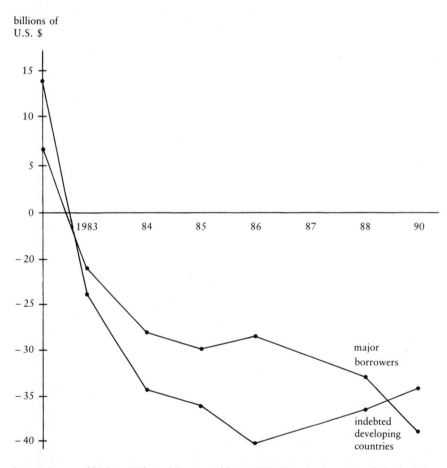

Source: Lever and Huhne, *Debt and Danger*, table 4. 1987–90 projections come from the International Monetary Fund.

Figure 6–5. Net Debt Transfer: Net New Borrowing Minus Interest, 1982–90

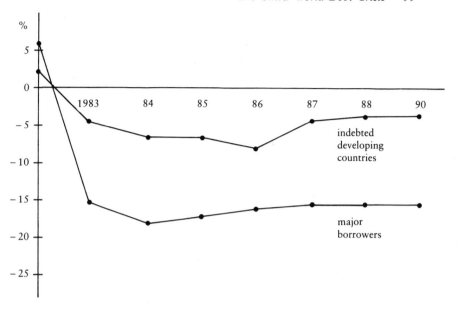

Source: 1982–86 data are derived from Lever and Huhne, *Debt and Danger*, table 4. 1987–90 projections come from the International Monetary Fund.

Figure 6–6. Net Debt Transfer as a Percentage of Exports, 1982–90

This would suggest that the debt crisis is far from over. In spite of some temporary calm throughout 1986 (except for Mexico's near default), policymakers and bankers can ill afford to ignore the problem. The international financial system is clearly not working for the long-term interests of either the advanced or the developing nations. How much longer can this go on? What can be done to solve this festering debt crisis?

While there are theoretical scenarios that would permit a degree of optimism for some of the more advanced industrializing countries—such as Argentina and Brazil—there is no conceivable scenario in which Mexico can survive its present dilemma. Mexico, we shall argue in the following chapter, is the weak link in the chain. When it snaps, the international financial system will be in a free-fall.

7
The Mexican Debt Crisis: A Case Study

The international economic situation strongly influences the problems of Mexico and Latin America. Our countries are suffering from an unprecedented financial and economic crisis. The rise in interest rates, the contraction of international trade and the protectionist measures adopted by industrialized nations constitute obstacles to our recovery. These factors also aggravate the social inequalities in the region and threaten the political stability of several Latin American nations. . . . It is Mexico's conviction, more and more generalized throughout the world, that in order to overcome the international crisis, the present framework of international economic relations must be modified toward a more cooperative structure in which national economic policies will be in tune with a global need to expand trade and reduce interest rates. . . . We are realistically facing the necessary internal reordering of our economies. What is required is that industrialized nations carry out coherent economic policies that avoid the transfer of costs of recovery to developing nations, and which set the basis for a more equal world economic order.[1]

—Miguel de la Madrid,
President of Mexico

The Mexican debt crisis is unique compared to those of most other developing debtor nations. Mexico is an oil exporter. It has over 72 billion barrels of proven petroleum reserves. How is it possible that a nation with such vast resource wealth can be one of the world's largest debtor nations? Certainly, Mexico's debt story is different from, for example, those of Argentina and Brazil. Therefore, Mexico, since it is a key player in the debt game, merits special attention.

By 1986, Mexico's total foreign debt totaled a staggering $98 billion. As is evident from figure 7–1, this increase in foreign debt was most rapid throughout the late 1970s and early 1980s. The total foreign debt in 1973 was less than $10 billion. It reached $50 billion by 1980. Then, in just five years, it nearly doubled. The skyrocketing of foreign debt in the early 1980s came in a period of prolonged economic stagnation in Mexico. As figure 7–2 indicates, during the 1980s Mexico has averaged an annual growth rate of real GDP of minus 4 percent.

What happened? By August 1982, a gradual decline in oil prices touched off a debt crisis resulting in the rescheduling of debt and the need for additional

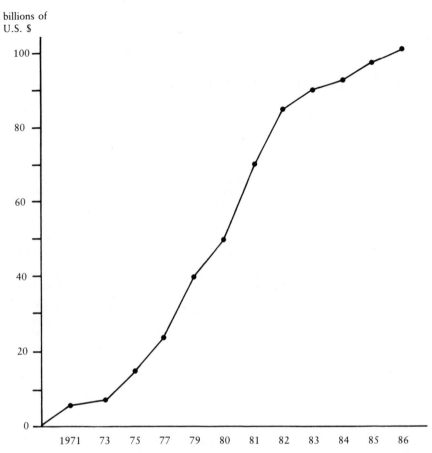

billions of
U.S. $

Source: 1970–85 data are derived from Morgan Guaranty Trust Co., Banco de Mexico, World Bank, and the United Nations. 1986 projection comes from the International Monetary Fund.

Figure 7–1. Mexico's Foreign Debt, 1970–86

loans to meet debt service obligations. To pay for this rescue operation, Mexico endured four years of strangling austerity that laid the groundwork for a near collapse in 1986.

Despite the 1983–86 global recovery, Mexico was worse off in 1986 than it was in 1982. Its gross domestic product declined by 5 percent in 1986 alone. Inflation in that year was estimated to be between 80 and 100 percent. Underemployment was nearly 50 percent, and the population growth rate approximately 3 percent. An economic growth rate of negative 5 percent coupled with a population growth rate of 3 percent means that in just one year, real per capita income fell by 8 percent. Since 1983, real wages have fallen by 50 percent, reducing the standard of living to levels of 1960.

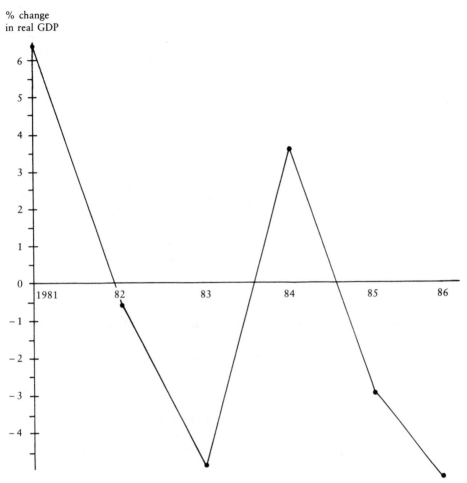

% change
in real GDP

Source: Inter-American Development Bank, Annual Report, 1986.

Figure 7–2. The Growth in Mexico's Real Gross Domestic Product, 1981–86

Mexico's total public and private external debt, nearly $100 billion, required over $14 billion in debt service payments in 1986. Of this amount, interest payments alone were $10 billion. Mexico earns about 75 percent of its foreign exchange from oil exports, but the collapse of oil prices in 1986 meant that Mexico would not earn enough to *even cover the interest* on its debt. The drop in oil prices produced a major decline in anticipated oil revenues—over $5 billion in 1986. Foreign exchange reserves dwindled to approximately $2.5 billion. The peso was systematically devalued. It reached a level of over 750 pesos to the U.S. dollar in 1986 compared to 22 pesos per dollar as recently as 1982.

Mexico's domestic budget deficit in 1986 was 13 percent of GDP. Interest payments on accumulated domestic public debt required over 70 percent of the annual federal budget, compared to 15 percent in the United States. Any way one looks at it, Mexico is virtually bankrupt. How can a semi-industrial developing nation with over 72 billion barrels of proven petroleum reserves be in such critical economic straits? It's an interesting, complicated, and unprecedented story.

Economic and Political Background

Mexico's economy experienced a sustained expansion between 1940 and 1960. It averaged 7 percent annual real growth during that period. But, in spite of some modernization of its agricultural and industrial sectors, the Mexican development path was characterized by great social and economic inequality and a structural dependence upon the United States for both trade and direct private foreign investment.

Politically, Mexico experienced great stability. Smooth transitions between presidents every six years were guaranteed by the dominant political party, the Revolutionary Institutional Party (PRI). The PRI had for decades successfully neutralized any genuine opposition. Its economic policies and programs contributed to the accumulation of private capital and wealth by an upper class tied to foreign capital. To maintain domestic stability, the PRI allocated resources to public works projects and some social services to maintain its political legitimacy. This model and strategy worked effectively until around 1968.

The closing years of the Diaz Ordaz administration were most notable for the Tlatelolco student massacre a few days before the 1968 Olympic games. Directed at the PRI, the student demonstrations and protests were for much-needed social and economic reforms.

Stage I. Failed Ambitions for Reform: 1968–76

It was President Luis Echeverria's primary goal during his 1970–76 administration to restore confidence in the PRI and make reforms to enhance the legitimacy of the state (for all intents and purposes, the PRI), while continuing to provide the necessary environment for the continued expansion and accumulation of capital. While real economic growth averaged 5.7 percent during his term in office, the Mexican economy by 1976 was in a deep and serious crisis (a fact that has been largely ignored by most recent studies on Mexico's current debt crisis).

Echeverria was committed to developing the rural sector, encouraging heavy industry for employment in the urban sector, improving education, implementing programs for the redistribution of income, and enhancing the popular participation of workers and peasants. To accomplish these goals, he greatly expanded the state (public) sector. In 1973, legislation was passed calling for foreign investment controls. This created not only a halt to the inflow of foreign capital but a flight of capital as well. Also in 1973, Mexico experienced earthquakes, floods, and the OPEC oil price increase. (It is important to recall that Mexico was a net importer of oil in 1973.)

The emerging economic crisis had its roots in the adverse international economic environment and the fiscal irresponsibility of the state sector. In the context of his goals and commitments, Echeverria spent well beyond Mexico's means. This resulted in the rapid rise of huge public deficits. These deficits were worsened by inflation, capital flight, declining foreign investment, and higher oil prices. The global recession of 1974–75 further depressed the Mexican economy, which is dependent on the U.S. market for over 66 percent of its exports.

By 1976, the economic crisis was severe. The growth of real GDP had fallen to 4.2 percent, compared to an average of 7 percent from 1972 to 1975. Inflation had soared to 15.8 percent compared to the 5 percent rates of 1971–72. Public expenditures had risen to 33.6 percent of GDP compared to 20.9 percent in 1971, when Echeverria took office. And, as a result, public sector deficits reached the level of 10 percent of GDP by 1976, compared to only 2.5 percent in 1971.

Stage II. Jose Lopez Portillo and Petroleum: 1976–82

Jose Lopez Portillo took over the Mexican presidency in 1976. Until the oil discovery in the following year, it appeared that his task was going to be implementing a difficult economic austerity program. But, the great oil find changed the picture entirely.

The discovery of an estimated 72 billion barrels of hydrocarbon reserves in 1977 temporarily rescued Mexico's faltering economy. Prior to this windfall, most experts agreed that no president could solve the structural problems of the economy. The discovery of petroleum changed the pattern of expectations dramatically. It now appeared that petroleum exports could be used to solve Mexico's economic and social problems. The vision of new sources of revenue triggered a debate over future development strategy and economic policy. A pervasive optimism and spirit of confidence swept across Mexico. Many experts argued that Mexico could manage its oil resources and wealth in a way that would avoid the distortions and contradictions that had plagued other oil-rich developing nations such as Iran, Nigeria, and Venezuela.

The government's goals were ambitious: an annual economic growth rate of 8 percent, increased public spending, enlargement of the private sector, the expansion of tourism and the agricultural sector, and, lastly, the rapid development of the petroleum sector. But, these goals and programs required an enormous amount of capital. Anticipating years of steady income from oil exports, Mexico began a spending and borrowing spree that continued unabated until 1982, when the bubble burst.

From 1977 to 1981, the development and exploitation of oil reserves was the principal stimulus for economic growth; yet it was at the same time the primary source of the emerging instability. The economy was continuing to grow—from 1978 to 1981, economic growth averaged 8.5 percent—but the internal inflationary pressures and the increasing external disequilibrium signaled the real costs of a petroleum-driven development strategy. While exports increased by 9 percent a year between 1978 and 1981, imports increased by 24 percent a year, a rate four times higher than the previous five-year average. The exports were, of course, primarily oil and gas—2.5 million barrels per day. As the manufactured goods export sector stagnated, the relative share of petroleum exports rose from 21 percent in 1977 to 71 percent in 1981, while manufacturing fell from 46 percent to 17 percent.

This structural shift was worsened by the deepening global recession, the weakening demand in the oil market, and the rapid increase in interest rates. The extent of the crisis was clearly visible in the deteriorating balance of payments, which registered a deficit of $13 billion in 1981. As projected oil revenues fell from $20 billion to $14 billion, Mexico's borrowing accelerated. External debt advanced to $68 billion in 1981 and to over $80 billion in 1982.

The unfavorable balance of payments position, accelerating inflation (from 29 percent in 1981 to 95 percent in 1982), and the mountain of foreign debt undermined all efforts to keep the exchange rate under control. An initial devaluation of the peso induced a panic prompting a massive flight of capital and an erosion of confidence in the government.

In virtual desperation, Lopez Portillo appointed Carlos Tello to direct the Mexican central bank in September 1982. Tello immediately set into motion an economic program which included: (1) the suspension of the convertibility of the peso, (2) strict controls on imports, (3) foreign exchange controls, and (4) the nationalization of Mexico's banks. This nationalist economic program emphasized a diversification of the economy even if it required protectionist and expansionary economic policies. Tello adopted a firm stance vis-à-vis the IMF during Mexico's loan negotiations. Tello objected to the IMF's devotion to traditional policy prescriptions requiring harsh austerity in stabilization programs. However, he soon left office.

Stage III. Miguel de la Madrid's Austerity Measures: 1983–86

On December 1, 1982, Miguel de la Madrid was inaugurated president. Tello was replaced by Jesus Silva Herzog who, as finance minister, was put in charge of economic policy. Upon taking office, de la Madrid refused to blame Mexico's economic crisis on declining oil prices and rising interest rates as Portillo had done during the final months of his term.

The new government set out to reverse Tello's policies and accommodate itself to the demands of the IMF. As the new economic program emerged, its essential features were: (1) a relaxation of foreign exchange controls so that the peso could float in the open market while a temporary official exchange rate would prevent further capital flight, (2) a request to restructure $20 billion of debt due between August 1982 and December 1984 (this request was tied to a new credit of $5 billion in addition to the IMF loan request of $3.2 billion), (3) an across-the-board increase in prices of goods and services provided by the government, and (4) a commitment to drastically reduce domestic spending.

The administration of Miguel de la Madrid also called for the moral regeneration of Mexico's leadership. A combination of economic belt-tightening measures and political measures to end corruption were implemented to improve Mexico's economic and political crises.

The IMF austerity measures put in place during 1983 produced some encouraging yet costly results. The public sector deficit was reduced from 18 percent of GDP to 9 percent, imports were reduced by 50 percent, and exports remained at their 1982 level of $21.3 billion. However, because of compounding, total debt service continued to grow at an increasing rate.

By fall 1984, the Mexican government reached an agreement with international bankers to reschedule its debt over a fourteen-year period. Mexico successfully followed IMF guidelines and signed an agreement with its 520 creditor banks to borrow an additional $3.8 billion. Also, about $12 billion in private sector debt was rescheduled.

If we carefully examine the growth of Mexico's public debt and debt service from 1973 to 1982, we can observe interesting, significant, and not commonly understood trends in new borrowing and debt service and their impact on net proceeds (the difference between new borrowing and debt service payments).

Figure 7–3 and table 7–1 show that since 1973, net new borrowing increased rapidly, as did total debt service. By 1978, debt service ($6.2 billion) exceeded new borrowing ($5.8 billion), and net proceeds became negative in 1979 ($4.5 billion) and in 1980 ($5.4 billion). Only a huge increase in new borrowing in 1981 ($8.6 billion) brought net proceeds back to a breakeven point. In August 1982, the Mexican economy collapsed and the nation could

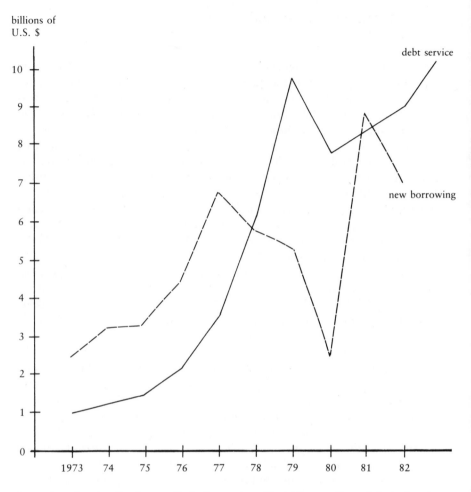

Source: Inter-American Development Bank, *Economic and Social Progress Report in Latin America*, 1984.

Figure 7–3. Mexico's New Borrowing and Debt Service, 1973–82

not meet its debt obligations. This precipitated a global recognition that there was the very real possibility of Mexico defaulting on its foreign debt.

As is shown in figure 7–3, there were a number of critical junctions for Mexico over this ten-year period. From 1973 to 1977, new borrowing increased, as did debt service payments. However, in 1977, new borrowing began to decline, but debt service continued to increase, creating an enormous gap between incoming funds from new borrowing and funds flowing out to pay accumulated interest and amortization. The massive increase in new

Table 7–1
Mexico's Debt, Debt Service, and Net Proceeds, 1973–83
(millions of U.S. $)

	Public Debt		Debt Service			Net Proceeds	Net Proceeds as a Percentage of New Borrowing
	Total (1)	New (2)[a]	Interest + (3)	Amortization (4)	= Total (5)	(2) − (5) (6)	[(2) − (5)]/(2) (7)
1973	7,249	2,444	358	795	1,154	1,290	53%
1974	10,517	3,268	572	624	1,196	2,072	63
1975	13,829	3,312	832	763	1,595	1,717	52
1976	18,291	4,462	1,087	1,154	2,241	2,221	48
1977	25,149	6,858	1,314	2,238	3,552	3,306	48
1978	30,970	5,821	1,818	4,408	6,226	− 405	− 7
1979	36,398	5,428	2,855	7,111	9,966	− 4,538	− 83
1980	38.911	2,513	3,842	4,026	7,868	− 5,355	− 213
1981	47,519	8,608	4,700	3,782	8,482	+ 126	.02
1982	54,963	7,304	5,892	3,072	8,964	− 1,660	− 23
1983	72,465	18,000	6,850	3,104	9,954	+ 8,046	+ 44

Source: Inter-American Development Bank, *Economic and Social Progress in Latin America, 1985 Report.*
Note: Figures may not add exactly due to rounding.
[a]Total new loans added to the foreign debt each year.

borrowing in 1981 was a desperate and unsuccessful attempt on the part of the Portillo administration to avert the crisis that everyone knew was coming.

But, even these figures are understated, because the large increases in new borrowing give the appearance of increasing net proceeds over the 1973–77 period. However, when taken *as a percentage of new borrowing,* net proceeds were *declining* over almost the entire decade even before they became negative in 1978, as illustrated in table 7–1. Therefore, the fact that the economy did collapse should not have been a surprise to anyone. Mexico had been running on a treadmill for at least five years before the 1982 collapse.

Looking at the evolution of Mexico's economic crisis in more conventional terms is just as revealing. Current account balance of payments data are supposed to measure a country's economic health. Looking at figure 7–4, for 1976–86, we can see that both the merchandise trade balance and the total current account balance were negative from 1976 to 1981. By 1981, the trade deficit reached $4.2 billion and the total current account deficit approximately doubled from its 1980 level of $7.5 billion to $14 billion. But, beginning in 1982, both the trade balance and the total current account showed an improvement. By 1984, the trade surplus was $12.8 billion and the current account surplus $2.5 billion.

This interesting turn of events came about because during the 1982–84 period, Mexico was following IMF guidelines by reducing imports and attempting to increase exports. The global recovery beginning in 1983 provided some

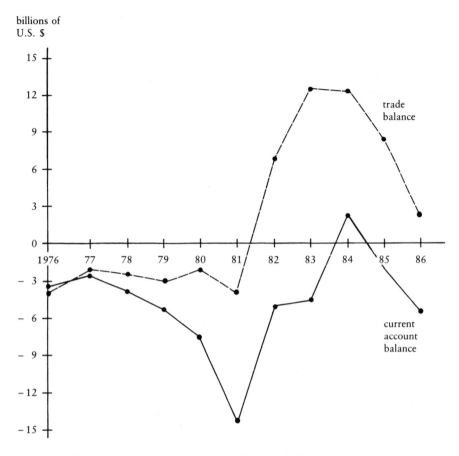

Source: Inter-American Development Bank, Annual Report, 1986.

Figure 7–4. Mexico's Trade Balance and Current Account Balance, 1976–86

stimulus, as did the systematic devaluation of the peso, which made Mexico's exports more competitive and imports more expensive. Mexico slowly began to adjust to moderately declining oil exports and reductions in anticipated oil revenues. But, by 1986, the trade balance dropped to only $2.6 billion and the current account deficit plunged to almost $5 billion.

In addition, capital flight continued from 1983 to 1985. Morgan Guaranty Trust Company estimated that $17 billion fled Mexico in those years, bringing total capital flight from 1976 to 1985 to a level of $53 billion or *almost one-half* of Mexico's total foreign debt.[2]

Table 7–2 summarizes the consequences of the chronic balance of payments deficit *and* the debt service burden. By 1982, Mexico's net payment to foreign capital was over $11 billion—28 percent of the total for Latin America.

Table 7-2
Mexico's Balance of Payments and Current Account, 1976–83
(billions of U.S. $)

	1976	1977	1978	1979	1980	1981	1982	1983
Merchandise trade (exports/imports)	−3.470	−.657	−1.745	−2.827	−2.307	−4.159	+6.793	+13.678
Net payment to foreign capital	−2.518	−2.506	−3.261	−4.579	−6.682	−10.055	−11.200	−9.395
Freight and insurance	−.300	−.296	−.418	−.607	−.946	−1.123	−.620	−.415
Dividends, interest, royalties, etc.	−2.218	−2.210	−2.843	−3.972	−5.736	−8.932	−10.581	−8.980
All other transactions	+1.329	−.191	+.191	+.226	+.275	+0	−.265	+.356
Balance current account	−3.410	−1.849	−3.162	−5.469	−7.537	−14.020	−4.878	−5.546
Net payment to foreign capital:								
All Latin America	−9.5	−11.2	−13.5	−17.4	−22.5	−31.5	−39.8	N.A.
Mexico as a percentage total Latin America	26%	22%	23%	26%	29%	32%	28%	N.A.

Source: Inter-American Development Bank, *Economic and Social Progress in Latin America, 1984 Report;* "The Two Faces of Third World Debt," *Monthly Review,* January 1984, p. 4.

(Payment to foreign capital is calculated by adding freight and insurance payments to dividends, interest, and royalties.) Between 1976 and 1982, Latin America's total *net* payment to foreign capital was $145 billion; of this Mexico alone had paid around $40 billion. This long-standing balance of payments disequilibrium in the face of the debt crisis fueled a vicious cycle and worsened the social and political contradictions that emanated from it.

As we pointed out earlier, in the late 1970s, private commercial banks began to play a larger role in international lending to sovereign states, as reflected in the changing composition of Mexico's debt. As a percentage of its total foreign debt, Mexico's debt obligations to private commercial banks increased to almost 92 percent by 1983, whereas debt from official sources decreased to a low of just over 8 percent.

Moreover, as Mexico became more and more dependent on private sources of credit, the terms of borrowing also changed. Mexico's percentage of debt at floating rates increased from 46.8 percent in the 1973–75 period to 82.4 percent in 1983. This increased dependence on commercial bank loans placed Mexico in a very precarious relationship with the U.S. government. As U.S. banks became more involved with Mexico's debt problem, Mexico's debt problem became more a concern for the U.S. government and financial community.

By March 1984, nine of the leading U.S. banks had a total of $14.5 billion in loans to Mexico. By June 1984, the 209 major U.S. banks had $26 billion in loans to Mexico—almost 25 percent of their total loans to major Third World debtor countries.[3] Consequently, they began to reduce their exposure. Looking at table 7–3, we can see that the banks reduced the amount of their primary capital as a percentage of loans considerably over the 1982–85 period. Citicorp,

Table 7–3
Exposure of Major U.S. Banks to Mexican Debt, 1982, 1985
(billions of $)

	1982		1985	
	Loans	Loans as a Percentage of Capital	Loans	Loans as a Percentage of Capital
Citicorp	$3.4	62%	$2.8	25%
Bank of America	2.5	51	2.7	37
Manufacturers Hanover	1.7	52	1.8	37
Chase Manhattan	1.4	37	1.7	28
Chemical	1.5	62	1.5	36
Bankers Trust	0.8	48	1.3	39
Morgan Guaranty	1.1	33	1.1	21
First Chicago	0.8	47	0.9	32
First Interstate	0.7	33	0.7	24
Wells Fargo	0.6	45	0.6	27

Source: Keefe, Bruyette & Woods.

for example, in 1982, had $3.4 billion in loans to Mexico, which represented 62 percent of its primary capital (shareholders equity plus allowance for loan losses). But, by 1985, Citicorp had reduced its exposure to Mexico to $2.8 billion, which represented only 25 percent of primary capital. U.S. banks reduced their total exposure in Mexico from 35 percent of primary capital in 1981 to 23 percent in 1985.

So, while the situation has improved somewhat, it is still precarious. If the top ten U.S. lenders to Mexico had not received any interest payments from Mexico in 1985, they would have suffered a pretax earnings reduction of 19 percent. This might be *temporarily* tolerable, but very soon such losses would certainly trigger a sequence of events that would create a financial panic, which is what almost occurred in 1986, when the collapse of oil prices (from $25 to $12.50 per barrel) again put Mexico on the brink of collapse and potential default. This sent a shock wave throughout the international financial system. Once again, Mexico needed a major rescue operation.

Stage IV. The 1986 Rescue Package

As Mexican oil revenues decreased from $14.7 billion in 1985 to under $6 billion in 1986, it was clear that Mexico could no longer meet its debt obligations. The 1986 crisis provoked widespread debate about the causes, consequences, and costs of the debt. A popular public point of view was that Mexico could not and should not have to face more years of harsh austerity just to satisfy the IMF and commercial bankers, but more conservative elements in the Mexican government felt that it was critical that Mexico meet the demands of the IMF and obtain the loans necessary to avoid a default. Others argued that the loans were necessary but felt that concessions should be made by the IMF and the international banking community. This faction maintained that Mexico had attempted to restructure its economy and had imposed austerity. The unfortunate collapse of oil prices in 1986, they insisted, should be a responsibility shared by the commercial banks and the international financial institutions.

By October 1986 the outline of a comprehensive new loan package was visible. In essence, it provided for loans of over $12 billion over the period 1986–87. As shown in table 7–4, the package involves all of the major players: the IMF, the World Bank, the Inter-American Development Bank, commercial banks, and the U.S. government.

Interestingly, this package appears to be consistent with U.S. Treasury Secretary Baker's Third World debt program. As the *Wall Street Journal* put it:

> The Baker plan . . . emphasized that the debt crisis could only be resolved through sustained growth by the debtor countries—that austerity alone would

Table 7–4
Mexican Loan Package
(millions of $)

Source	1986	1987	Total
International Monetary Fund	$ 700	$ 900	$ 1,600
World Bank	900	1,000	1,900
Inter-American			
Development Bank	200	200	400
Commercial banks[a]	2,500	3,500	6,000
International export credits	500	1,000	1,500
U.S. farm credits	200	600	800
Total	$5,000	$7,000	$12,200

Source: U.S. Treasury, June 22, 1986.
[a]Not yet agreed to.

be self-defeating in the longer run. To achieve the requisite growth, the plan proscribed orthodox programs of economic reform and structural adjustment for the debtor countries, including greater reliance on the private sector, curtailment of state subsidies and price controls, measures to stimulate both foreign and domestic investment, and export promotion and trade liberalization. The plan also called on private banks and multilateral institutions to step up sharply their lending to the indebted countries. The banks were urged to provide new commercial credits of $20 billion over a three-year period while the World Bank and the Inter-American Development Bank would contribute an additional $9 billion in loans.[4]

The proposed rescue package called for the commercial banks to generate approximately $6 billion in new loans. The IMF and World Bank loans were contingent on the commercial bank loans being secured. This package also contained some concessions for Mexico. The World Bank agreed to provide additional credit if real economic growth is less than 3.5 percent in 1987. The IMF loan of $1.6 billion guaranteed additional credit if oil prices fall below $9 per barrel. In exchange for this jumbo loan package, the IMF required Mexico to continue to sell off and reduce the number of state-owned enterprises, to liberalize trade, to attract more foreign investment, and to reduce its domestic deficit by 3 percent of GDP.

As of early October 1986, the real question was the willingness of the commercial banks to extend additional loans of this magnitude and to make interest rate concessions. Obviously, most have not been very anxious to do so, nor have they been happy about being cajoled by the monetary authorities to commit to new risky loans. But, on the other hand, if they do not provide the additional liquidity, Mexico will not be able to service its debt and the banks will face the consequences of a possible default.

This loan package will probably be in place by the end of 1986; nevertheless, it has come under severe criticism. Critics charge that it will only address the short-run problem of servicing immediate debt obligations. It will possibly get Mexico through 1987, assuming that the economy generates strong real growth, that oil prices stiffen or even increase, that the global economy continues to grow, and that interest rates do not rise—all questionable assumptions.

Critics assert that adding another $12 billion to Mexico's debt will merely increase the nation's long-term debt service obligations. More importantly, they argue that this loan package will not reverse the negative transfer of capital *from* Mexico *to* the advanced nations. Instead, it will merely perpetuate the negative flow. The critics also warn that this package will simply draw U.S. banks further into the debt quagmire. Moreover, they argue that the Mexican people should not have to suffer through more years of austerity and a further decline in their already low standard of living.

Reductions in government spending have left the economy and its people in a state of shock. *Que nos pasa?* (What has happened to us?) has become the slogan of the Mexican people. Political unrest is reaching dangerous proportions. Even if the economy did begin to generate real economic growth, that would, at best, only allow Mexico to service its debt. It would not confront the increasingly serious development needs of the nation.

Many critics of the debt-rescue programs are urging more drastic and unconventional responses on the part of the Mexican government. Following the lead of Alan Garcia, Peru's young president, who has stated that Peru will only pay 10 percent of Peru's export earnings for foreign debt service, there have been proposals urging Mexico to adopt a similar policy or, at least, to tie debt service payments to the level of oil prices.

Others, following the exhortation of Fidel Castro, have suggested that Mexico default on its debt rather than continue to hopelessly try to service foreign debt at such great social, political, and economic costs. Proponents of this view have carefully considered the consequences of such an action and have concluded that the benefits of default actually outweigh the disadvantages.

There is, in fact, a strong argument that the consequences of a unilateral governmental debt default on the part of a debtor country like Mexico are not as serious as is commonly thought. *London Times* financial correspondent Anatole Kaletsky has argued persuasively in *The Costs of Default* (1985) that governments actually stand to lose very little by unilaterally defaulting on foreign debts. In contrast to a business bankruptcy—the common analogy—government assets cannot be seized, and, after a default, trade would go on as usual. If anything, he argues, a government relieved of its debt obligations would probably have a better credit rating than before.

Thus, as Arthur MacEwan, an economist from the University of Massachusetts—Boston, has argued, it is puzzling that Mexico has not in fact taken this option given the apparent economic advantages. Yet, even MacEwan is quick to point out that, for political reasons, such a default is an unlikely scenario for Mexico. The more conservative members of the government and financial communities in Mexico, he argues, are not likely to permit a unilateral default. As members of the dominant upper class in Mexico, they enjoy many economic and financial benefits from the debt expansion/debt service cycle in spite of the overall costs to the society as a whole.[5]

An Alternative Debt Strategy

Assuming that a default is not a politically viable or likely option—given the present political climate—what then could Mexico do other than continue to walk the debt treadmill? The basic principles of any genuine long-term solution to Mexico's debt crisis must make five guarantees. (1) The reforms must be adequate in scope to end the negative capital flow from Mexico to the advanced industrialized countries. (2) Any new money loaned to Mexico must be used for productive investment which increases capital formation and the competitive productive capability of the nation. (3) Any new lending should come primarily from private commercial banks. (4) A system of regulating new commercial bank flows to Mexico must be established. (5) There must be a formal arrangement between Mexico's monetary authorities, the U.S. Federal Reserve, and commercial banks to reduce capital flight. The primary objective of these principles would be to insure a long-term solution based upon a sustainable system of financial flows.[6]

The first step toward a viable alternative debt plan would be for Mexico to privately agree to a "conciliatory default," a premeditated action in which everyone agrees that the debt cannot be fully repaid and that a new approach must be tried. This could be called a major rescheduling. Following this, the present level of interest payments would be reduced by rescheduling. The remainder would be paid for by new voluntary commercial bank lending that would be guaranteed by the U.S. government. Such a guarantee on loans would be conditional on the banks writing down each year for a period of five years a percentage of the existing debt judged to be nonperforming, that is, not servicing even interest payments.[7]

The IMF would need to support this strategy. This would require a change in philosophy and orientation to accommodate the Mexican situation. Mexico needs to have a growth strategy to produce its way out of the debt crisis. It cannot continue to accept externally imposed austerity. The political and economic costs are too high. The IMF, working with the World Bank and the Inter-American Development Bank, could play a more positive role by allowing Mexico more flexible domestic monetary and fiscal policies. This flexibility could take on the character of the recent experiences in Argentina and Brazil. For the most part, this would allow Mexico the opportunity to implement monetary reform combined with a wage and price freeze in order to halt inflationary pressures while confronting the debt crisis at the same time.

In addition, the World Bank and the Inter-American Development Bank could significantly increase their capitalization in order to allocate larger amounts of development assistance to Mexico. This would alleviate some of the pressure being placed upon a very limited federal budget. It may, in fact, be possible for the World Bank to actually cofinance and guarantee some of the new loans to Mexico.

Mexico realized several years ago that it needed to restructure its economy. Controls on capital flight, privatization of inefficient and corrupt state-controlled industries, a lowering of trade barriers, tax reform, and price controls have been instituted or are being considered.[8] Most of these reforms, however, will not be politically possible without a significant reduction and eventual elimination of the debt burden. A major rescheduling or a long-term debt moratorium (like a chapter 11 bankruptcy filing in the United States) would guarantee Mexico a fresh start and some hope of success. The alternative of further economic austerity will eventually tear the country apart politically and have disastrous consequences for U.S.–Mexican relations.

Most experts agree that political reforms, income redistribution, and real economic growth are necessary for Mexico to survive. It is not politically feasible, though, to expect the government and people of Mexico to achieve these goals while running on a debt treadmill. Without a fundamental resolution of the debt problem, long-term goals such as economic growth benefitting the entire population, authentic development, and genuine democracy will remain elusive.[9]

8

The Future: More Debt Crises?

The U.S. Economy in Transition: The Late 1980s

The Reagan supply-side revolution produced mixed results for the domestic economy. The deep and prolonged recession between 1981 and 1983 brought inflation down to almost zero. The easing of monetary policy beginning in 1983 caused interest rates to fall to relatively low levels. Yet, in spite of some positive indicators, overall economic growth has been weak. Unemployment is intractably stuck at a historically high 7 percent rate. Investment spending is down. GNP growth is below 3 percent. The federal deficit is growing larger and larger, hitting a record high of $230 billion in 1986. The public debt is over $2 trillion, requiring over 15 percent of the federal budget to service the interest alone.

The international economic situation for the United States further complicates a fragile and lackluster domestic economy. The trade deficit in 1986 reached a record $170 billion. The foreign exchange value of the dollar has gradually fallen, but little agreement exists within the administration about how low it should be allowed to fall. As interest rates decline, it is more and more possible that there will be a halt in the flow to the United States of foreign money (chasing safe and attractive rates of return) which has been in part financing the trade and budget deficits. This halt would force the United States to finance its own trade and budget deficits. In addition, the growing burden of financing the U.S. external debt is beginning to have a significant drag on the U.S. economy.

In a speech before the 64th annual meeting of the Banker's Association for Foreign Trade in May 1986, E. Gerald Corrigan (president of the Federal Reserve Bank of New York) made the following points about the U.S. international economic situation:

> It is a virtual certainty that the net external indebtedness of the U.S. will approach one-half trillion dollars by the end of the decade, constituting not only a heavy mortgage on future generations, but also implying external debt servicing costs that will make it all the more difficult to approach a current account balance even in the long run.

The simultaneous presence in the U.S. of lingering inflationary expectations and a rising level of domestic demand and investment in the face of massive budget deficits clearly helped produce a situation in which nominal and real interest rates were quite high. . . . That situation, together with the associated huge domestic savings gap, made a strong dollar both inevitable and, ironically, necessary.

In some very important respects we have been fortunate that the recent drop in the dollar exchange rate has not seemed to materially impair the willingness of foreigners to increase their holdings in dollar-denominated assets.

An improvement in the U.S. trade position with the other industrial countries can come about only if higher rates of GNP growth in those countries are also accompanied by still higher rates of growth in their domestic demand.

Whether viewed from the perspective of domestic inflation, growth in the world economy, or growth in the world trading system, greater export expansion offers a more promising approach than does suppressed imports.

I would hasten to emphasize again that the solution to our external problems cannot come from the exchange rate alone and, as a related point, that in the current setting, we must be especially sensitive to the dangers of overshooting on the downside—the consequences of which could be quite severe.

The wrong way [to maintain trade surpluses in the LDCs] is via artificial import restraints which can only stand in the way of needed structural reforms; the right way is in the context of more open and growing economies in which exports are rising, but so too are imports, including imports from the United States.[1]

U.S. International Economic Policy

The Reagan administration has consistently advocated a position of encouraging free trade and avoiding a drift toward protectionism. The economic recovery that began in 1983, along with falling worldwide prices for oil and other commodities, have had positive effects on the U.S. economy in the short run.

Since 1985, the Reagan administration has been appealing to West Germany and Japan in particular to stimulate their economies by cutting taxes and interest rates. If this were to happen, the Reagan administration argues, U.S. exports would increase and the trade deficit would decline. But, West Germany and Japan are fearful of worsening their own budget deficits and inflation problems.

Of course, as we have seen, the theoretical rhetoric is that balanced trade benefits everyone. But, in the case of the United States, the huge budget deficit makes the goal of balanced trade difficult, if not impossible. Despite the declines in U.S. interest rates and the dollar's exchange value, the trade deficit is still staggering. Interest rates are still relatively high and continue to lure foreign money which finances the U.S. trade and budget deficit.

The September 1985 Plaza Agreement (resulting in a decision by the Group of Five to push the dollar down by internationally concerted interventions in the foreign exchange market) has produced mixed results. While intervention throughout 1986 drove the dollar down, improvement in the trade deficit has not resulted. And, worse, according to Robert D. Hormmats, a vice president of Goldman, Sachs and Company, "The harmony which characterized last September's Plaza Hotel agreement to lower the dollar has turned to acrimony over trade, exchange rates and demands for changes in domestic policies."[2]

Lindley H. Clark, Jr., writing for the *Wall Street Journal* in August 1986, assessed the Plaza Agreement accordingly:

> The Reagan administration has offered some rhetoric about closer coordination of international economic policies, but so far it has been a lot of talk and very little action. Closer coordination would require that major countries agree on where they want to go. Right now there is no indication that they even agree on where we are.
>
> The decline of the dollar obviously hasn't been the magic solution to U.S. trade problems that many people expected, so the Treasury thinks the next step is to push the dollar down farther. Fed Chairman Paul Volcker worries that further declines in the dollar could lead to increasing inflation, not an altogether groundless fear.[3]

Clark concluded his analysis by arguing that the success of fixed exchange rates depends on international cooperation, but that the Group of Five's efforts illustrate that countries cooperate only when they believe it's in their own individual self-interest.

In October 1986, the members of the IMF and the World Bank held their annual meeting in Washington, D.C. President Reagan addressed the participants and asserted that, "The only ways to resolve the external imbalances between countries are through increased growth abroad, a greater competitiveness for the U.S. dollar or both, coupled with the opening of markets."

While the Reagan administration talked of the need for cooperation and coordination of domestic economic policies, the West Germans and Japanese once again balked at following the directives issued by the United States. As Leonard Silk, economic journalist for the *New York Times,* pointed out, "The stalemate over economic growth, interest rates and exchange rates . . . is likely to continue. For the policy differences are deep and, at this juncture, seem irreconcilable."[4]

West Germany and Japan, in defense of their position, charge that the U.S. budgetary disorder is the major problem and that President Reagan has done nothing to address it and its international consequences. In spite of the inability of the leaders from the major Western governments to agree on policy, there was one fact that they could agree on—that the world economy is headed for serious trouble unless constructive action is taken soon. This is quite clear in the following excerpt from the major address given by J. de Larosière, managing director of the International Monetary Fund.

> There is always the temptation to respond to unexpected short-term changes with short-term policy adjustments. In some cases, these adjustments are necessary. But we must not forget that the attempt to fine-tune economic management is fraught with difficulty.
>
> A delicate but decisive transition is under way. It is a transition from stop–go policies and inflationary expansion to a program of monetary and fiscal stability aimed at sustained growth. A good start has been made. But persistence and international cooperation are now required to insure that the needed growth occurs, while further progress is made in removing imbalances.
>
> For their part, the developing countries can best improve their growth performance and their access to credit markets by their choice of macroeconomic and structural policies.
>
> Significant progress has been made over the past few years. Economic policies are now better attuned to economic realities, and inflation—which had been poisoning the financial system for fifteen years—has finally been brought under control in the industrial world.
>
> But much remains to be done. External payments imbalances among the larger industrial countries are a disturbing source of instability and tensions. The erosion of commodity prices has adversely affected the developing countries at the very time when they more than ever need increased export earnings to grow and to service their debts.
>
> In a world that is increasingly interdependent, it is proving more complex than ever to cope with these problems. A satisfactory solution requires not only an understanding of the interaction among national economic policies but also firm adherence to the fundamental principle of monetary stability and strengthened commitment to international cooperation.
>
> Economic policy coordination among industrial countries is no longer a matter of theoretical preference. It is instead a prerequisite for growth with stability. Industrial countries must work together to complete the process of disinflation, to maximize the sources of economic growth, and to assure an open international trading system.[5]

The Triple Debt Crisis: The Limits of Orthodox Policy

Gerald Epstein, an economist from The New School for Social Research in New York City, has argued that there is a triple debt crisis—the U.S. budget deficit, the U.S. trade deficit, and the Third World debt crisis. As he points out:

> These three crises . . . have the world economy in a serious bind. World economic growth is necessary to solve these problems, but world economic growth seems to be out of reach—largely because of the troublesome and paralyzing ways in which these debts interact with the dollar problem.[6]

As reflected in figure 8–1, this conceptualization of the problem raises serious questions about the ability of orthodox economic policy to resolve these problems.

Looking back upon recent U.S. monetary and fiscal policies, it is easy to see why. In essence, the Fed's tight money policy in the early 1980s and Reagan's loose fiscal policy have generated this triple debt crisis. It was Reagan's huge tax cut coupled with massive military expansion that resulted in record budget deficits. Meanwhile, the Federal Reserve's tight monetary policy produced high interest rates and an overvalued dollar, which decreased the competitiveness of U.S. exports and increased the U.S. trade deficit. To continue financing these trade deficits and the federal deficit, the United States was able to attract foreign investment only by keeping interest rates high. But, in the process, the United States became a debtor nation. Finally, Volcker and Reagan's strategy of maintaining an overvalued dollar and high interest rates dramatically increased the

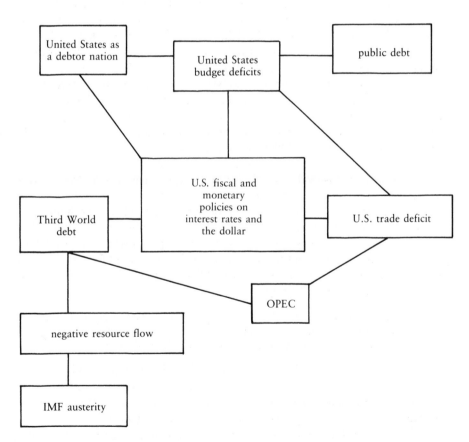

Figure 8–1. The Triple Debt Crisis

debt-servicing burdens of Third World countries, thereby worsening the international debt crisis.[7]

The contradictions emerging from the interrelationships between these three major problems have made it almost impossible for conventional policy to address them. Because of the large federal deficit, the United States has needed a large flow of foreign money to finance this debt. In order to attract foreign money, the United States has had to keep real interest rates high. But, high real interest rates stimulate demand for the dollar; thus, the dollar becomes overvalued and the U.S. trade deficit increases. The high real interest rates tend to restrain economic growth, but economic growth is needed to increase the U.S. trade balance. As the trade deficit increases, the United States needs even higher real interest rates to maintain the increased flow of foreign capital. And on it goes. This is what Epstein has called a "vicious cycle of economic sabotage."[8]

As this cycle repeats itself, the international debt crisis also worsens. The high real interest rates merely increase the debt-servicing burden of debtor nations. To facilitate a solution for the debt crisis, it is imperative that the United States generate strong economic growth and lower interest rates. Yet, because of the international role of the dollar, the United States is being forced to maintain high real interest rates and accept a slowdown in economic growth. If the United States significantly reduced the budget deficit, it is likely that economic growth would slow even more. Or, if the Fed opted for a very easy monetary policy and allowed interest rates to fall further, a dollar crisis would probably result, as the demand for dollars would fall dramatically.

The complexity of today's triple debt crisis has presented policymakers with a set of seemingly unsolvable problems. Most experts have concluded that this is the time to fundamentally reconsider the role of the dollar in the international monetary system. Others add that the structure and behavior of multinational financial institutions have greatly increased the international mobility of capital. This rapid movement of capital seeking its highest rate of return in unregulated international financial markets has worsened the problems of the international monetary system. Howard Wachtel has argued this point with regard to "supranational" firms.

> The supranational economy, therefore, consists of banks and corporations that conduct their economic affairs beyond the political reach of national governments, which are confined to specific geographic boundaries.[9]

Therefore, Wachtel concludes that a transnational policy strategy is now needed to deal with the new problems created by an integrated private world economy beyond the reach of domestic economic policymakers and international political mechanisms capable of exercising economic management.

While the problem of the role of the U.S. dollar and the mobility of capital in the context of a supranational global economy are the critical issues of our time, it is beyond the scope of this book to examine solutions for each problem. It is important to note that there have been some thoughtful proposals.[10] Most involve a comprehensive strategy for international reconstruction. In essence, such a program involves: reducing the role of the U.S. dollar, implementing significant debt relief for Third World debtor nations, formally coordinating the economic policies of the major industrial countries, and developing pragmatic regulations governing the mobility of capital across national boundaries.

The post–World War II history of the international monetary system can only be understood from the vantage point of the role of the U.S. dollar. This history is, in fact, a story of the dollar.

This book has developed this history in the context of the basic theories of international trade and finance. The international economic problems of the 1970s and 1980s have been examined. No solution appears to be on the horizon, only competing analytical perspectives. The only thing that is certain is that the domestic and international economic problems confronting the United States are serious, requiring wisdom and strong leadership to avert economic disaster.

Reprinted by permission: Tribune Media Services.

Notes

Chapter 2
The Role of International Trade

1. *Dollars and Sense,* March 1986, p. 14.
2. Thomas Riddell, Jean Shackelford, and Steve Stamos, *Economics: A Tool for Understanding Society,* Instructor's Manual (Reading, Mass.: Addison-Wesley, 1982), Chapter 13.
3. *Dollars and Sense,* March 1986, p. 15.
4. *New York Times,* August 3, 1986.
5. *U.S.A. Today,* February 14, 1986.
6. *U.S.A. Today,* November 7, 1986.
7. *Wall Street Journal,* June 19, 1986.

Chapter 4
International Finance

The data used in this chapter came from the following principal sources: *The Economic Report of the President,* 1986; *The Survey of Current Business,* July 1986; *The International Monetary Fund,* Annual Report, 1985; and the Citibase data tape from Citicorp, 1985.

Chapter 5
The U.S. Debt Crisis

1. Center for Popular Economics, *Economic Report of the People* (Boston: South End Press, 1986), Chapter 7, "Trouble in Farm Country," pp. 93–114.
2. Ibid.
3. John B. Judis, *In These Times,* July 23, 1986, pp. 7–8.
4. Ibid.
5. Statement of Donald T. Regan, as Secretary of the Treasury, before the House Banking, Finance and Urban Affairs Committee, Washington, D.C., Dec. 21, 1982.

6. Howard M. Wachtel, *The Money Mandarins* (New York: Pantheon Books, 1986), pp. 107–108.

Chapter 6
The Third World Debt Crisis

1. John C. Pool and Stephen C. Stamos, Jr., "The Uneasy Calm: Third World Debt," *Monthly Review*, March 1985, p. 8.
2. The real interest rate is the difference between the nominal interest rate and the rate of inflation.
3. The interest rate most commonly used for international loans is the London Inter-Bank Offered Rate, which varies daily. Most international loans are made at 7/8 percent above the LIBOR rate.
4. Loans to developing countries can be stated as a percentage of primary capital or the equity held by shareholders. As the percentage of potentially nonperforming loans increases in comparison to its capital, the bank becomes increasingly vulnerable should the debt not be repaid in full or repudiated, i.e., not paid in full.

Chapter 7
The Mexican Debt Crisis: A Case Study

This chapter is a revised and expanded version of our article "The Uneasy Calm: Third World Debt," *Monthly Review*, March 1985, pp. 7–20.

1. Miguel de la Madrid, "Mexico: The New Challenges," *Foreign Affairs*, Fall 1984, pp. 62–76.
2. Morgan Guaranty Trust Company, "LDC Capital Flight," *World Financial Markets*, March 1986, pp. 13–15.
3. Anatole Kaletsky, *The Costs of Default* (New York: Priority Press, 1985), p. 113, Table 6.4.
4. Peter Hakim, "The Baker Plan: Unfulfilled Promises," *Challenge*, September–October 1986, pp. 55–59; James A. Baker III, Secretary of the Treasury, Statement before the Committee on Foreign Relations, U.S. Senate, October 23, 1985.
5. Arthur MacEwan, "Latin America: Why Not Default?," *Monthly Review*, September 1986, pp. 1–13.
6. Harold Lever and Christopher Huhne, *Debt and Danger: The World Financial Crisis* (Boston: The Atlantic Monthly Press, 1985), pp. 120–136.
7. John C. Pool and Stephen C. Stamos, Jr., "Devising a Bankruptcy Plan for Mexico," *New York Times*, Sunday, Business Forum, June 8, 1986.
8. Pedro Aspe, "Charting Mexico's Economic Progress," *Wall Street Journal*, August 8, 1986; U.S. Department of the Treasury, "Mexico's Program for Sustained Economic Growth," July 22, 1986.
9. Jorge Castaneda, "Mexico at the Brink," *Foreign Affairs*, Fall 1985, pp. 287–303.

Chapter 8
The Future: More Debt Crises?

1. E. Gerald Corrigan, "Reducing International Imbalances in an Interdependent World," *Quarterly Review,* The Federal Reserve Bank of New York, Spring 1986, Vol. 11, No. 1, pp. 1–5.

2. Robert D. Hormatts, "Can Teamwork Help Us Avert Global Depression?," *New York Times,* August 15, 1986.

3. Lindly H. Clark, Jr., "How the Group of Five Buried Fixed Exchange Rates," *Wall Street Journal,* August 19, 1986.

4. Leonard Silk, "Reagan's Plea to the Allies," *New York Times,* October 1, 1986.

5. *New York Times,* October 1, 1986.

6. Gerald Epstein, "The Triple Debt Crisis," *World Policy,* Fall 1985, Vol. II, No. 4, p. 626.

7. Ibid., p. 643.

8. Ibid., p. 636.

9. Howard Wachtel, *The Money Mandarins* (New York: Pantheon, 1986), pp. 4–5.

10. See Epstein, "The Triple Debt Crisis," which includes Epstein's program for international reconstruction, and Wachtel, "Public Policy for a Supranational Order," in *The Money Mandarins* (chapter 9).

Suggested Bibliography

Robert Z. Aliber, *The International Money Game,* fourth edition (New York: Basic Books, 1979).

Fred Block, *The Origins of International Economic Disorder* (Berkeley: University of California Press, 1977).

Center for Popular Economics, *Economic Report of the People* (Boston: South End Press, 1986), chapter 11.

William R. Cline, *International Debt and the Stability of the World Economy* (Cambridge: MIT Press, 1983).

Committee on Energy and Commerce, U.S. House of Representatives, *The U.S. in a Changing World Economy: The Case for an Integrated Domestic and International Commercial Policy* (Washington, D.C.: Government Printing Office, 1983).

Gerald Epstein, "The Triple Debt Crisis," *World Policy,* Vol. II, No. 4, Fall 1985.

Inter-American Development Bank, *Economic and Social Progress in Latin America: External Debt: Crisis and Adjustment* (Washington, D.C.: Inter-American Development Bank, 1985).

International Monetary Fund, *World Economic Outlook* (Washington, D.C.: International Monetary Fund, 1986).

Anatole Kaletsky, *The Costs of Default* (New York: Priority Press, 1985).

Henry Kaufman, Sylvia Hewlett, and Peter Kenen, editors, *The Global Repercussions of U.S. Monetary and Fiscal Policy* (Cambridge: Ballinger, 1984).

Charles Kindleberger, *Manias, Panics, and Crashes* (New York: Basic Books, 1978).

Robert Z. Lawrence, *Can America Compete?* (Washington, D.C.: Brookings Institution, 1984).

Harold Lever and Christopher Huhne, *Debt and Danger: The World Financial Crisis* (New York: Atlantic Monthly Press, 1985).

John H. Makin, *The Global Debt Crisis: America's Growing Involvement* (New York: Basic Books, 1984).

Stephen Marris, *Deficits and the Dollar: The World Economy at Risk* (Washington, D.C.: Institute for International Economics, 1985).

Michael Moffit, "Economic Decline, Reagan Style: Dollars, Debt, and Deflation," *World Policy,* Vol. II, No. 3, Summer 1985.

Robert Pirog and Stephen C. Stamos, Jr. *Energy Economics: Theory and Policy* (Englewood Cliffs, N.J.: Prentice-Hall, 1987).

John Pool and Ross LaRoe, *The Instant Economist* (Reading, Mass.: Addison-Wesley, 1985).

Robert B. Reich, *The Next American Frontier* (New York: Times Books, 1983).

Thomas Riddell, Jean Shackelford, and Stephen Stamos, *Economics: A Tool for Understanding Society,* third edition (Reading, Mass.: Addison-Wesley, 1987).

Alan Riding, *Distant Neighbors: A Portrait of the Mexicans* (New York: Knopf, 1985).

Anthony Sampson, *The Money Lenders: The People and Politics of the World Banking Crisis* (London: Penguin Books, 1981).

Susan Strange, *International Economic Relations of the Western World 1959–1971* (New York: Oxford University Press, 1976).

U.S. Government, *Mexico: A Country Study* (Foreign Area Studies Series (Washington, D.C.: Government Printing Office, 1985).

Howard Wachtel, *The Money Mandarins: The Making of a Supranational Economic Order* (New York: Pantheon, 1986).

Miguel S. Wionczek, editor, *Politics and Economics of External Debt Crisis: The Latin American Experience* (Boulder, Colo.: Westview, 1985).

World Bank, *World Development Report 1985: International Capital and Economic Development* (New York: Oxford University Press, 1986).

Index

About the Authors

John Charles Pool received his B.A. and M.B.A. from the University of Missouri and his Ph.D. in economics from the University of Colorado. He is coauthor of *Economia: Enfoque America Latina* (McGraw-Hill, 1982) and *The Instant Economist* (Addison-Wesley, 1985) and author of *Studying and Thinking about Economics and Society* (Addison-Wesley, 1986), and he has published numerous articles on various topics in economics. He also writes (with Ross M. LaRoe) a syndicated newspaper column, "The Instant Economist," which treats current issues in economics. Dr. Pool has taught at Bucknell University and the Universities of Iowa and Missouri. For two years, he was a Fulbright Professor in Mexico. Currently, he is an adjunct professor of economics at St. John Fisher College. He is head of Charles Pool & Associates in Rochester, New York, a firm specializing in research and writing in the field of managerial and international economics.

Steve Stamos received his B.A. from San Diego State University, his M.S. in economics from Wright State University, and his Ph.D. in political economy from the Union Graduate School. He is coauthor of *Economics: A Tool for Understanding Society* (Addison-Wesley, third edition, 1986) and *Energy Economics: Theory and Policy* (Prentice-Hall, 1986). He has published widely in professional journals on the topics of energy and international economics. Dr. Stamos has been associate professor of economics at Bucknell University since 1974. In addition, he has been a visiting professor at Evergreen State College and the University of Massachusetts-Amherst and a consultant to various public and private agencies. He is also associated with Charles Pool & Associates, Rochester, New York.

Dr. Pool and Dr. Stamos have collaborated on several studies of Latin American economic issues, including major analyses of Mexican external debt and the role of tourism in the Mexican economy. They have both lived and taught in Mexico.